THE **100+** SERIES™

Reproducible Activities

Math

Grades 7-8

Published by Instructional Fair
an imprint of
Frank Schaffer Publications®

Instructional Fair

Editors: Melissa Warner Hale, Christopher Kjaer

Frank Schaffer Publications®

Instructional Fair is an imprint of Frank Schaffer Publications.

Send all inquiries to:
Frank Schaffer Publications
8720 Orion Place
Columbus, Ohio 43240-2111

Math—grades 7–8

ISBN: 0-7424-1723-9

5 6 7 8 9 10 11 MAZ 10 09 08 07 06

Table of Contents

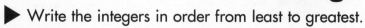

Integers

► Write the integers in order from least to greatest.

1. 50, 2, ⁻40, ⁻48, 39, ⁻10, 15, ⁻39

_____

3. ⁻3,012, ⁻2,891, ⁻4,560, ⁻3,201, ⁻4,559, ⁻2,999, ⁻3,021, ⁻5,472

_____

► Write *T* if the number sentence is true. Write *F* if it is false.

3. -5 + 7 = 7 + -5 _____   **4.** ⁻9 + ⁻3 = ⁻3 + ⁻9 _____

5. ⁻6 – ⁻4 = ⁻4 – ⁻6 _____   **6.** 4 – ⁻2 = ⁻2 – 4 _____

7. ⁻31 + 135 = 135 + ⁻31 _____   **8.** ⁻88 – 22 = 22 – ⁻88 _____

► The **commutative property** says the order of the values can be switched without changing the answer.

9. Is addition of integers commutative? That is, does *a* + *b* = *b* + *a* for all integers *a* and *b*?

10. Is subtraction of integers commutative? That is, does *a* – *b* = *b* – *a* for all integers *a* and *b*?

11. Try changing the order of the numerals in several multiplication problems with integers. Is multiplication of integers commutative?

12. Try changing the order of the numerals in several division problems with integers. Is division of integers commutative?

Addition and Subtraction with Integers

▶ To complete each square, add across and subtract down.

1. + →

-5	4	
-8	2	

2. + →

-6	2	
-1	-2	

3. + →

7	-3	
5	-6	

4. + →

-3	-4	
4	-2	

5. + →

-4	-2	-6
6	1	

6. + →

	1	-8
	1	-3
	5	

7. + →

-1	-6	-7
-3	-2	

8. + →

-4	5	
2		0

Multiplication and Division with Integers

▶ Write an integer in each square so the statements across and down are correct.

1.

	x		=	8
x	■	x	■	x
⁻1	x		=	
=	■	=	■	=
⁻2	x		=	32

2.

24	÷		=	
÷	■	x	■	÷
	x	3	=	
=	■	=	■	=
⁻6	÷		=	2

Integers and Exponents

$(-2)^4$ means "take -2 to the fourth power."
-2^4 means "find the opposite of 2 to the fourth power."

$(-2)^4 = (-2) \times (-2) \times (-2) \times (-2)$ $-2^4 = -(2 \times 2 \times 2 \times 2)$
$= 4 \times 4 = 16$ $= -(4 \times 4) = -16$

▶ Find the value of each number.

1. $(^-5)^2$　　　　　　　**2.** $^-3^3$　　　　　　　**3.** $^-4^2$

4. $(^-3)^2$　　　　　　　**5.** $^-2^6$　　　　　　　**6.** $(^-8)^4$

7. $(^-4)^2$　　　　　　　**8.** $^-5^2$　　　　　　　**9.** $(^-9)^2$

A **negative exponent** means take the reciprocal and then take the power.

$$2^{-3} = (\tfrac{1}{2})^3 = \tfrac{1}{2} \times \tfrac{1}{2} \times \tfrac{1}{2} = \tfrac{1}{8}$$

$$(^-4)^{-3} = (-\tfrac{1}{4})^3 = -\tfrac{1}{4} \times -\tfrac{1}{4} \times -\tfrac{1}{4} = -\tfrac{1}{64}$$

▶ Find the value of each number.

10. 5^{-2}　　　　　　　**11.** 3^{-3}　　　　　　　**12.** $(-5)^{-3}$

13. $(-2)^{-5}$　　　　　　**14.** $(-3)^{-4}$　　　　　　**15.** 6^{-2}

7   0-7424-1723-9 *Math*

Integers in Context

Integers include the positive and negative counting numbers.

Jenna borrowed $4 on Tuesday, and then borrowed $7 on Thursday. How much does she owe in all? Equation: $^-4 + {}^-7 = n$ Solution: $n = -11$. Jenna owes $11 in all.	From a 4 foot diving platform, a diver jumps up 3 ft. and then falls 18 ft. before touching the bottom of the pool. How deep is the pool? Equation: $4 + 3 + {}^-17 = m$ Solution: $m = {}^-10$ ft. The pool is 10 feet deep.

► Write and solve a number sentence that fits each situation.

1. Todd borrowed $5 for lunch. His allowance is $15. How much does he have left after paying back what he owed?

2. A scuba diver descended 25 ft. below sea level, rose 8 ft., and then descended 12 ft. At what depth was the diver?

3. On a board game, Luisa rolled a 7. She drew a card that said to move back 8 spaces. That square told her to move ahead 4 spaces. How far did Luisa end up away from her starting position?

4. Kiyoshi bought a $150 stereo on a payment plan. He made a down payment of $70. What is his credit balance?

Name _____

Date _____

Equivalent Fractions

How many days did the longest sneezing fit last?

 ▲ Shade in the boxes that contain equivalent fractions to get the answer.

$\frac{14}{16}=\frac{7}{8}$	$\frac{5}{6}=\frac{20}{24}$	$\frac{4}{10}=\frac{2}{5}$	$\frac{2}{11}=\frac{10}{44}$	$\frac{5}{9}=\frac{10}{18}$	$\frac{4}{16}=\frac{1}{4}$	$\frac{8}{12}=\frac{2}{3}$	$\frac{10}{7}=1\frac{4}{7}$	$\frac{15}{6}=2\frac{1}{2}$	$\frac{20}{8}=2\frac{1}{2}$	$\frac{33}{22}=1\frac{1}{2}$
$\frac{1}{5}=\frac{10}{50}$	$\frac{20}{24}=\frac{2}{13}$	$\frac{3}{7}=\frac{18}{42}$	$\frac{10}{60}=\frac{2}{15}$	$\frac{6}{14}=\frac{3}{8}$	$\frac{16}{42}=\frac{2}{5}$	$\frac{2}{11}=\frac{6}{33}$	$\frac{18}{5}=3\frac{3}{5}$	$\frac{20}{4}=5$	$\frac{54}{14}=3\frac{9}{14}$	$\frac{30}{7}=4\frac{2}{7}$
$\frac{4}{15}=\frac{16}{60}$	$\frac{32}{100}=\frac{8}{25}$	$\frac{1}{4}=\frac{8}{32}$	$\frac{12}{26}=\frac{3}{8}$	$\frac{4}{10}=\frac{20}{60}$	$\frac{5}{7}=\frac{15}{35}$	$\frac{5}{40}=\frac{1}{8}$	$\frac{48}{14}=2\frac{3}{7}$	$\frac{49}{21}=2\frac{1}{3}$	$\frac{35}{28}=1\frac{1}{4}$	$6=\frac{18}{3}$
$\frac{10}{35}=\frac{2}{5}$	$\frac{3}{14}=\frac{9}{44}$	$\frac{4}{50}=\frac{2}{25}$	$\frac{1}{2}=\frac{17}{35}$	$\frac{7}{32}=\frac{1}{4}$	$\frac{14}{30}=\frac{2}{5}$	$\frac{3}{7}=\frac{15}{35}$	$\frac{37}{2}=17\frac{1}{2}$	$\frac{42}{21}=2$	$\frac{8}{5}=1\frac{2}{5}$	$\frac{36}{13}=2\frac{10}{13}$
$\frac{6}{8}=\frac{16}{24}$	$\frac{14}{16}=\frac{3}{4}$	$\frac{12}{30}=\frac{2}{5}$	$\frac{6}{34}=\frac{3}{16}$	$\frac{4}{6}=\frac{8}{14}$	$\frac{3}{4}=\frac{9}{16}$	$\frac{10}{25}=\frac{2}{5}$	$\frac{17}{3}=3\frac{1}{3}$	$\frac{22}{5}=4\frac{2}{5}$	$\frac{10}{4}=2\frac{1}{2}$	$\frac{40}{7}=5\frac{5}{7}$

0-7424-1723-9 *Math*

Comparing Fractions

The city of Madrid experienced a 23-hour-long traffic jam. Why were the police so excited that they took time off from work?

▶ Read each statement. If the statement is incorrect, cross out that letter. The letters that are left will give the answer.

$\frac{3}{4} < \frac{4}{5}$	$\frac{5}{12} < \frac{7}{18}$	$\frac{6}{7} < \frac{7}{6}$	$\frac{1}{4} > \frac{3}{12}$	$\frac{5}{6} > \frac{4}{5}$	$3\frac{5}{8} < \frac{30}{8}$	$\frac{2}{10} > \frac{1}{11}$
S	E	P	L	A	I	N
$\frac{4}{12} < \frac{3}{10}$	$14\frac{1}{2} < \frac{33}{2}$	$\frac{5}{8} < \frac{6}{10}$	$\frac{8}{10} < \frac{7}{9}$	$\frac{5}{3} > \frac{3}{2}$	$\frac{6}{3} < 3\frac{1}{2}$	$\frac{2}{3} < \frac{13}{20}$
B	W	A	C	O	N	K
$\frac{8}{9} > \frac{17}{21}$	$\frac{1}{2} < \frac{1}{4}$	$\frac{3}{5} > \frac{8}{13}$	$\frac{17}{40} > \frac{2}{5}$	$5\frac{1}{3} < \frac{14}{3}$	$2\frac{1}{4} < \frac{5}{2}$	$\frac{5}{7} < \frac{5}{8}$
T	D	F	H	I	E	J
$\frac{11}{24} > \frac{18}{42}$	$\frac{1}{5} > \frac{5}{20}$	$\frac{4}{7} < \frac{15}{21}$	$\frac{16}{3} < \frac{34}{6}$	$\frac{9}{20} > \frac{17}{35}$	$\frac{6}{33} < \frac{2}{10}$	$\frac{5}{18} < \frac{3}{9}$
W	G	O	R	M	L	D
$\frac{7}{32} < \frac{6}{31}$	$\frac{12}{21} > \frac{5}{7}$	$\frac{10}{60} < \frac{10}{12}$	$\frac{6}{15} > \frac{1}{5}$	$\frac{16}{20} > 1$	$4\frac{1}{3} < \frac{8}{2}$	$7\frac{1}{5} > \frac{21}{5}$
N	P	C	U	T	V	P

Adding Fractions

▶ Add the fractions and write your answer
in simplest form. Show your work.

1. $\dfrac{3}{5} + \dfrac{1}{4} =$

2. $\dfrac{17}{20} + \dfrac{1}{4} =$

3. $\dfrac{7}{10} + \dfrac{2}{15} =$

4. $\dfrac{3}{8} + \dfrac{2}{3} =$

5. $\dfrac{4}{7} + \dfrac{2}{9} =$

6. $\dfrac{13}{35} + \dfrac{19}{50} =$

7. $1\dfrac{5}{8} + 6 =$

8. $2\dfrac{1}{3} + 1\dfrac{7}{18} =$

9. $2\dfrac{11}{12} + 4\dfrac{5}{6} =$

10. $\dfrac{1}{3} + 3\dfrac{5}{7} =$

11. $5\dfrac{4}{9} + 7\dfrac{17}{18} =$

12. $4\dfrac{5}{8} + 6\dfrac{1}{2} =$

13. $\dfrac{11}{13} + 1\dfrac{5}{12} =$

14. $3\dfrac{8}{15} + 1\dfrac{9}{20} =$

15. $\dfrac{4}{5} + 3\dfrac{7}{8} =$

Subtracting Fractions

Which U.S. city is known as Celery City?

▶ Subtract. Write the letter for each answer below.

L. $\dfrac{7}{10} - \dfrac{1}{3} =$ **A.** $\dfrac{3}{5} - \dfrac{1}{4} =$ **O.** $\dfrac{5}{6} - \dfrac{1}{2} =$

I. $\dfrac{4}{5} - \dfrac{3}{10} =$ **A.** $\dfrac{17}{18} - \dfrac{7}{9} =$ **A.** $\dfrac{13}{15} - \dfrac{1}{5} =$

M. $\dfrac{17}{20} - \dfrac{7}{30} =$ **I.** $\dfrac{21}{25} - \dfrac{3}{5} =$ **N.** $\dfrac{5}{8} - \dfrac{3}{16} =$

O. $\dfrac{3}{4} - \dfrac{7}{16} =$ **A.** $\dfrac{4}{5} - \dfrac{2}{7} =$ **H.** $\dfrac{7}{8} - \dfrac{3}{12} =$ **G.** $\dfrac{17}{20} - \dfrac{3}{5} =$

K. $3\dfrac{5}{8} - 2\dfrac{3}{4} =$ **M.** $15\dfrac{3}{4} - 12\dfrac{8}{9} =$ **Z.** $1\dfrac{3}{4} - \dfrac{7}{10} =$ **C.** $\dfrac{7}{12} - \dfrac{2}{5} =$

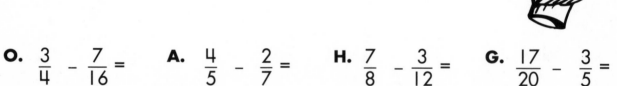

$\dfrac{7}{8}$	$\dfrac{18}{35}$	$\dfrac{11}{30}$	$\dfrac{2}{3}$	$\dfrac{37}{60}$	$\dfrac{7}{20}$	$1\dfrac{1}{20}$	$\dfrac{1}{3}$	$\dfrac{5}{16}$

$2\dfrac{31}{36}$	$\dfrac{6}{25}$	$3\dfrac{11}{60}$	$\dfrac{5}{8}$	$\dfrac{1}{2}$	$\dfrac{1}{4}$	$\dfrac{1}{6}$	$\dfrac{7}{16}$

0-7424-1723-9 *Math*

Multiplying Fractions

▶ Multiply. Write the answer in lowest terms.

1. $\dfrac{15}{32} \times \dfrac{4}{5} =$

2. $\dfrac{2}{3} \times \dfrac{4}{5} =$

3. $\dfrac{5}{14} \times \dfrac{21}{25} =$

4. $\dfrac{21}{40} \times \dfrac{16}{35} =$

5. $\dfrac{10}{47} \times \dfrac{21}{40} =$

6. $\dfrac{11}{20} \times 30 =$

7. $\dfrac{7}{45} \times 55 =$

8. $80 \times \dfrac{61}{70} =$

9. $\dfrac{111}{132} \times 60 =$

10. $49 \times \dfrac{17}{21} =$

11. $3\dfrac{11}{18} \times 6\dfrac{3}{10} =$

12. $3\dfrac{1}{9} \times 4\dfrac{1}{8} =$

13. $2\dfrac{14}{25} \times 5\dfrac{5}{12} =$

14. $11\dfrac{1}{5} \times 5\dfrac{5}{6} =$

15. $2\dfrac{20}{21} \times 1\dfrac{7}{8} =$

0-7424-1723-9 *Math*

Dividing Fractions

What do the emu, the cassowary, and the ostrich have in common?

▶ Divide. Write the problem letter above its answer each time it appears.

F. $8 \div \frac{2}{3} =$ **B.** $16 \div \frac{12}{13} =$

Y. $21 \div 3\frac{1}{3} =$ **H.** $35 \div 4\frac{1}{6} =$

D. $\frac{7}{11} \div \frac{3}{5} =$ **C.** $\frac{1}{4} \div \frac{3}{10} =$

A. $\frac{2}{3} \div \frac{1}{4} =$ **T.** $\frac{3}{7} \div \frac{5}{6} =$ **E.** $\frac{1}{3} \div \frac{4}{9} =$ **R.** $\frac{5}{6} \div \frac{4}{5} =$

L. $56\frac{2}{5} \div 8\frac{6}{13} =$ **N.** $41\frac{1}{3} \div 11\frac{7}{5} =$ **I.** $4\frac{3}{20} \div 3\frac{5}{6} =$ **S.** $6\frac{2}{5} \div 1\frac{3}{7} =$

$\frac{18}{35}$	$8\frac{2}{5}$	$\frac{3}{4}$	$6\frac{3}{10}$		$2\frac{2}{3}$	$1\frac{1}{24}$	$\frac{3}{4}$

$17\frac{1}{3}$	$1\frac{19}{230}$	$1\frac{1}{24}$	$1\frac{2}{33}$	$4\frac{12}{25}$		$\frac{18}{35}$	$8\frac{2}{5}$	$2\frac{2}{3}$	$\frac{18}{35}$

,

$\frac{5}{6}$	$2\frac{2}{3}$	$3\frac{1}{3}$	$\frac{18}{35}$		12	$6\frac{183}{275}$	$6\frac{3}{10}$

!

     0-7424-1723-9 *Math*

Estimating Mixed Number Sums and Differences

▶ Each frog represents an estimated sum or difference. Write the letter of the correct lily pad problem next to each frog.

1. _____ 12

2. _____ 17

3. _____ 11

4. _____ 22

5. _____ 18

6. _____ 21

A. $10\frac{8}{11} + 11\frac{5}{11} =$

D. $5\frac{2}{3} + 5\frac{7}{10} =$

B. $31\frac{4}{9} - 12\frac{5}{6} =$

E. $33\frac{5}{12} - 12\frac{3}{7} =$

C. $14\frac{2}{5} + 3\frac{3}{8} =$

F. $17\frac{3}{4} - 6\frac{3}{5} =$

0-7424-1723-9 *Math*

Estimating Mixed Number Products and Quotients

▶ Estimate a whole number answer for each problem.

1. $8\frac{5}{8} \times 9\frac{1}{3} =$

2. $59\frac{7}{12} \div 4\frac{5}{8} =$

3. $12\frac{7}{11} \times 3\frac{3}{10} =$

4. $1\frac{11}{20} \times 13\frac{11}{18} =$

5. $12\frac{3}{7} \times 4\frac{6}{11} =$

6. $56\frac{2}{5} \div 8\frac{6}{13} =$

7. $44\frac{7}{16} \div 11\frac{7}{15} =$

8. $44\frac{13}{20} \div 3\frac{5}{14} =$

9. $36\frac{2}{5} \div 1\frac{4}{7} =$

10. $63\frac{2}{9} \div 6\frac{7}{10} =$

11. $8\frac{6}{11} \times 6\frac{8}{15} =$

12. $7\frac{7}{10} \times 5\frac{3}{8} =$

0-7424-1723-9 *Math*

Fractions and Exponents

If the exponent is outside the parenthesis, the entire fraction should be raised to the power.

$$\left(\frac{4}{5}\right)^3 = \frac{4}{5} \times \frac{4}{5} \times \frac{4}{5} = \frac{64}{125}$$

If only a part of the fraction is raised to a power, then only that number is raised to the power.

$$\frac{4^3}{5} = \frac{4 \times 4 \times 4}{5} = \frac{64}{5} = 12\frac{4}{5}$$

A negative exponent means take the reciprocal and then take the power.

$$\left(\frac{4}{5}\right)^{-3} = \left(\frac{5}{4}\right)^3 = \frac{5}{4} \times \frac{5}{4} \times \frac{5}{4} = \frac{125}{64} = 1\frac{61}{64}$$

▶ Write each of the following fractions in simplest form.

1. $\left(\dfrac{5}{6}\right)^2$

2. $\left(\dfrac{8}{9}\right)^2$

3. $\dfrac{2^2}{3}$

4. $\left(\dfrac{9}{10}\right)^2$

5. $\left(\dfrac{2}{3}\right)^3$

6. $\left(\dfrac{1}{2}\right)^5$

7. $\dfrac{3^2}{8}$

8. $\dfrac{3^3}{4}$

9. $\left(\dfrac{5}{7}\right)^2$

10. $\left(\dfrac{3}{4}\right)^3$

11. $\left(\dfrac{5}{6}\right)^{-2}$

12. $\left(\dfrac{5}{7}\right)^{-2}$

13. $\left(\dfrac{2}{3}\right)^{-3}$

14. $\left(\dfrac{1}{2}\right)^{-5}$

15. $\left(\dfrac{9}{10}\right)^{-2}$

Fractions and the Associative Property

An operation is **associative** if you can change the grouping of the numbers and still get the same result.

▶ Find the answers. Then, next to each problem number, write the letter of the expression that gives the same answer. Not all letter choices will be used.

____ **1.** $\left(\frac{1}{3} + \frac{2}{3}\right) + \frac{1}{2}$ ____ **2.** $\frac{3}{5} \times \left(\frac{2}{5} \times 8\frac{1}{2}\right)$ ____ **3.** $\frac{4}{5} \times \left(1\frac{1}{4} \times \frac{2}{3}\right)$

____ **4.** $\left(\frac{4}{7} + \frac{3}{14}\right) + \frac{5}{21}$ ____ **5.** $\left(\frac{5}{6} + \frac{1}{12}\right) + \frac{3}{24}$ ____ **6.** $\left(\frac{8}{9} \times \frac{18}{64}\right) \times 1\frac{17}{21}$

A. $\left(\frac{4}{5} \times 1\frac{1}{4}\right) \times \frac{2}{3}$ **B.** $\frac{8}{9} \times \left(\frac{18}{64} \div 1\frac{7}{21}\right)$ **C.** $\frac{3}{5} \div \left(\frac{2}{5} \times 8\frac{1}{2}\right)$

D. $\left(\frac{1}{3} + \frac{2}{3}\right) - \frac{1}{2}$ **E.** $\frac{4}{7} + \left(\frac{3}{14} + \frac{5}{21}\right)$ **F.** $\frac{5}{6} + \left(\frac{1}{12} + \frac{3}{24}\right)$

G. $\frac{3}{5} \times \left(\frac{2}{5} \div 8\frac{1}{2}\right)$ **H.** $\frac{1}{3} + \left(\frac{2}{3} + \frac{1}{2}\right)$ **I.** $\left(\frac{3}{5} \times \frac{2}{5}\right) \times 8\frac{1}{2}$

J. $\left(\frac{4}{5} + 1\frac{1}{4}\right) \times \frac{2}{3}$ **K.** $\frac{4}{7} + \left(\frac{3}{14} \times \frac{5}{21}\right)$ **L.** $\frac{8}{9} \times \left(\frac{18}{64} \times 1\frac{17}{21}\right)$

▶ Look for patterns in the matching problems above. Then complete these rules, where a, b, and c are fractions.

7. $(a + b) + c =$ _____

8. $a \times (b \times c) =$ _____

Fractions in Context

1. Karen wanted to buy a pair of jeans. They were on sale
for $\frac{1}{3}$ off the original price of $39.95. What was the
discount? How much did the jeans cost?

2. A board was 3 ft. $2\frac{7}{8}$ in. long, which turned out to be
$1\frac{3}{4}$ in. too long. How long was the board once $1\frac{3}{4}$ in.
was taken off?

3. Molly's closet had an area of $6\frac{1}{2}$ square feet. Her mom
expanded the closet, adding another $3\frac{5}{12}$ square feet.
Now what is the area of her closet?

4. Copeland put his full backpack on a scale. It weighed 16
lb. He took out three books and weighed it again. It now
weighed $12\frac{3}{4}$ lb. If each of the books was the same
weight, how much did each weigh?

5. A birthday cake was cut into 12 pieces. Seven people
each had one piece. The next day, $\frac{2}{3}$ of the remaining
cake was eaten. What portion of the original cake was
left?

Name _____

Date _____

Decimals and Place Value

What do you call a smart pig?

▲ Write the word name for each underlined number. When you are done, read the circled letters from top to bottom.

62.0567̲8 = ___ ___ ___ ___ ___ ⃝ ___ ___

1.00399̲8 = ___ ___ ___ ⃝ ___ ___

0.41 2̲65 = ___ ___ ___ ___ ___ ___

905.0436̲1 = ___ ___ ⃝ ___ ___ ___

23.2̲5775 = ___ ⃝ ___ ___ ___ ___

6.66579̲1 = ___ ___ ___ ___ ___ ⃝ ___ ⃝ ___

5,138.09̲687 = ___ ___ ___ ___ ⃝ ___

11,897.54600̲2 = ___ ___ ___ ___ ___ ⃝ ___

Reading and Writing Decimals

▶ Write the numeral for each number. (Hint: Decimal points take up their own square and leading zeros before a decimal are not included.)

DOWN

1. thirty-two and sixty-seven thousand, ninety-four hundred-thousandths
2. nine hundred eighteen and four hundred seventy six thousand, six hundred thirty-two millionths
3. two and two hundred ninety-nine thousandths
4. five hundred eight thousand, fifty-six millionths
5. seventeen hundred-thousandths
9. seven hundred five and thirty thousand, six hundred thirty-six hundred-thousandths
11. six hundred ten and two thousand, three hundred twelve millionths
12. seventy-four and nine thousand, three hundred one ten-thousandths

ACROSS

6. five hundred twenty-four and one hundred three thousand, eight hundred twelve millionths
7. eighty-seven and seventy-five thousand, thirty-four hundred-thousandths.
8. six thousand, three hundred thirty-four ten-thousandths
10. ten and six hundred eight thousand, two hundred eleven millionths
13. thirty-seven and four thousand, eight millionths
14. thirty-six and nine thousand, nine hundred ninety-two hundred-thousandths

Name_____ Date _____

Comparing and Ordering Decimals

Who claims credit for designing the American flag?

▶ Cross out the letters if the inequalities are incorrect.

A. 426.882345 > 426.8823445

B. 0.000018 > 0.00018

C. 1.336789 < 1.336799

D. 29.011377 < 29.010377

E. 9.99999 > 9.999999

F. 88.450001 > 88.045001

G. 5.801181 < 5.801118

H. 713.713317 < 731.713317

I. 4,665.801226 < 4,665.812126

J. 0.004422 < 0.004224

K. 2.200022 > 2.020022

L. 55.06673 > 55.06763

M. 3.199789 > 3.199879

N. 48,001.200121 < 48,001.201021 < 48,010.201112

O. 9,095.046689 < 9,095.046889 < 9,095.046899

P. 12,139.055065 > 12,139.055056 > 12,039.055056

Q. 922.011066 < 922.001086 < 9201.0011061

R. 0.454454 < 0.454554 < 0.4545554

S. 39.887887 > 39.887878 > 39.878887

T. 1,002.5668136 > 1,002.5668316 > 1,002.5668361

T	F	B	R	A	N	D	Q	G	M	C	I	E	S
E	M	J	H	O	P	L	K	I	T	N	S	O	N

22

0-7424-1723-9 *Math*

Rounding Decimals

Only which mosquitoes bite?

▶ To find out, follow the directions below.

1. Put an E above number 2 if 3.5968415 rounded to
the nearest thousandth is 3.597.

2. Put an A above number 1 if 23.451255 rounded to
the nearest ten-thousandth is 23.45126.

3. Put an O above number 5 if 649.3400007 rounded
to the nearest hundred-thousandth is 649.340001.

4. Put an E above number 6 if 2.19086 rounded to the nearest hundredth is 2.19.

5. Put an M above number 1 if 0.3888 rounded to the nearest tenth is 0.04.

6. Put a C above number 5 if 57.86 rounded to the nearest ten is 57.9.

7. Put a D above number 3 if 4.35506609 rounded to the nearest millionth is 4.355067.

8. Put an A above number 4 if 6.200009 rounded to the
nearest tenth is 6.2.

9. Put an L above number 5 if 88.231596 rounded to the
nearest thousandth is 88.232.

10. Put a B above number 2 if 375.75375 rounded to the
nearest hundred is 375.75.

11. Put an M above number 3 if 5.0663794 rounded to the
nearest millionth is 5.066379.

12. Put a D above number 6 if 44.689448 rounded to the
nearest ten-thousandth is 44.6694.

13. Put an F above number 1 if 382.8642402 rounded to the
nearest hundred-thousandth is 382.86424.

___ ___ ___ ___ ___ ___
 1   2   3   4   5   6

Adding and Subtracting Decimals

On which mission did astronauts return safely to Earth after an explosion damaged their spacecraft and prevented them from landing on the moon?

▶ Find the sums and differences. Write each problem letter above its answer.

A. 26.84403 + 39.70459   **N.** 39.92 + 45.51   **L.** 15.199 + 7.31

T. 540.62 – 17.91   **R.** 2.0005 – 0.9999   **I.** 631.02 – 583.4044

L. 16.982 + 15.19   **P.** 322.96 – 19.982   **O.** 612.98 – 43.301

E. 182.91 + 62.29   **H.** 98.83 – 62.019   **E.** 421.053 + 16.59

O. 198.6 – 23   **T.** 50 – 37.952

| ——— | ——— | ——— | ——— | ——— | ——— |
| 66.54862 | 302.978 | 175.6 | 22.509 | 32.172 | 569.679 |

| ——— | ——— | ——— | ——— | ——— | ——— | ——— | ——— |
| 12.048 | 36.811 | 47.6156 | 1.0006 | 522.71 | 245.2 | 437.643 | 85.43 |

Multiplying Decimals

▶ Multiply.

1.
$$\begin{array}{r} 0.438 \\ \times\ 0.177 \\ \hline \end{array}$$

2.
$$\begin{array}{r} 0.039 \\ \times\ 0.009 \\ \hline \end{array}$$

3.
$$\begin{array}{r} 0.246 \\ \times\ 0.183 \\ \hline \end{array}$$

4.
$$\begin{array}{r} 0.1211 \\ \times\ 0.344 \\ \hline \end{array}$$

5.
$$\begin{array}{r} 0.4768 \\ \times\ 0.189 \\ \hline \end{array}$$

6.
$$\begin{array}{r} 0.502 \\ \times\ 0.176 \\ \hline \end{array}$$

7.
$$\begin{array}{r} 0.0056 \\ \times\ 0.999 \\ \hline \end{array}$$

8.
$$\begin{array}{r} 0.317 \\ \times\ 0.02 \\ \hline \end{array}$$

9.
$$\begin{array}{r} 0.4951 \\ \times\ 0.113 \\ \hline \end{array}$$

10.
$$\begin{array}{r} 0.621 \\ \times\ 0.118 \\ \hline \end{array}$$

11.
$$\begin{array}{r} 0.088 \\ \times\ 0.029 \\ \hline \end{array}$$

12.
$$\begin{array}{r} 0.3551 \\ \times\ 0.208 \\ \hline \end{array}$$

Name_____ Date _____

Dividing Decimals

Which mammals get sunburned?

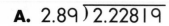

▶ Divide. Write the letter above its answer.

A. 2.89 ⟌ 2.22819

A. 0.81 ⟌ 43.254

H. 0.09 ⟌ 0.004806

I. 0.09 ⟌ 0.00558

N. 12.4 ⟌ 9.45004

D. 0.305 ⟌ 0.024766

N. 7.6 ⟌ 379.012

U. 2.63 ⟌ 21.34771

M. 1.9 ⟌ 9.4734

G. 41.8 ⟌ 1185.866

S. 0.63 ⟌ 0.0398286

S. 0.018 ⟌ 16.9776

P. 5.9 ⟌ 5.2097

| 0.0534 | 8.117 | 4.986 | 53.4 | 0.7621 | 943.2 |

| 0.771 | 49.87 | 0.0812 | | 0.883 | 0.062 | 28.37 | 0.06322 |

0-7424-1723-9 *Math*

Estimating Decimal Sums and Differences

What are baby kangaroos called?

▶ Follow the directions below.

1. Put a Y above number 5 if the estimated sum of 923.562 and 188.73 is 1,000.

2. Put an E above number 2 if the estimated difference between 9.369 and 0.849 is 9.

3. Put an L above number 1 if the estimated difference between 83.1106 and 26.004 is 60.

4. Put an A above number 4 if the estimated sum of 38.624 and 12.411 is 60.

5. Put an S above number 5 if the estimated sum of 777.772 and 521.86 is 1,300.

6. Put a T above number 3 if the estimated difference between 8.4956 and 5.823 is 3.

7. Put an N above number 3 if the estimated sum of 93.426 and 54.813 is 130.

8. Put an O above number 2 if the estimated difference between 7.643 and 1.53126 is 6.

9. Put a Y above number 4 if the estimated difference between 553.403 and 424.89 is 200.

10. Put a T above number 5 if the estimated sum of 66.3724 and 13.905 is 70.

11. Put a J above number 1 if the estimated sum of 8.1642 and 4.46 is 12.

12. Put an M above number 4 if the estimated difference between 410.366 and 262.887 is 200.

13. Put an E above number 3 if the estimated sum of 64.62 and 46.325 is 110.

14. Put a T above number 1 if the estimated difference between 454.919 and 132.9122 is 200.

____ ____ ____ ____ ____
  1   2   3   4   5

Estimating Decimal Products and Quotients

▶ Write the letter of the correct estimated product or quotient next to the problem.

_____ **1.** 40,107.81 ÷ 79.62　　　　　　　　　**A.** 90

_____ **2.** 49.67 x 531.2　　　　　　　　　**B.** 36,000

_____ **3.** 4,982.62 ÷ 47.1　　　　　　　　　**C.** 1,750

_____ **4.** 245.81 ÷ 5.161　　　　　　　　　**D.** 50

5.343

_____ **5.** 741.3 x 32.615　　　　　　　　　**E.** 21,000

_____ **6.** 24.98 x 66.35　　　　　　　　　**F.** 100

_____ **7.** 6.343 x 5,876.5　　　　　　　　　**G.** 500

1.12

_____ **8.** 77.642 x 34.41　　　　　　　　　**H.** 25,000

_____ **9.** 35,572.11 ÷ 421.12　　　　　　　　**I.** 2,400

Managing a Checking Account

▶ The spreadsheet shows transactions from a checking account. A withdrawal occurs when you pay a bill or take money out of the account. A deposit represents money that is put into the account. The balance is how much money you have in the account at that point. An overdraft occurs when you do not have enough money in the account for the withdrawal. Banks usually charge fees for overdrafts.

Trans. #	Date	Item	Withdrawal	Deposit	Balance
	10/1				$1,378.98
1	10/1	Rent	$1,050.00		$328.98
2	10/3	Groceries	$223.42		
3	10/3	Cash	$40.00		
4	10/5	Phone Bill	$36.30		
5	10/7	Car Payment	$178.46		
6	10/7	Overdraft Fee	$30.00		
7	10/8	Pay Check		$523.81	
8	10/10	Birthday		$30.00	
9	10/12	Electric Bill	$48.23		
10	10/15	Car Insurance	$298.60		
11					
12					

▶ Write a number sentence for the ten transactions shown above. Then, write the balance in the table. The first transaction has been done for you.

1. $1,378.98 − $1,050.00 = $328.98   6.

2.   7.

3.   8.

4.   9.

5.   10.

▶ Fill in the spreadsheet for each transaction below. Be sure to write in the new balance after each transaction.

11. Buy something on October 16 that will not cause an overdraft (a negative value).

12. You receive another paycheck on October 22.

Scientific Notation

What is a gathering of foxes called?

▶ Follow the directions below.

1. Write an A above number 2 if 8,136,000,000 equals 81.36×10^9.

2. Write a K above number 5 if 4.08×10^{-10} equals 0.000000000408.

3. Write a T above number 1 if 0.000000000000569 equals 5.69×10^{13}.

4. Write an L above number 6 if 9.7138×10^8 equals 97,138,000.

5. Write a K above number 2 if 772,600,000,000 equals 7.726×10^{11}.

6. Write an R above number 3 if 3.052×10^5 equals 0.00003052.

7. Write an E above number 7 if 1.004×10^8 equals 100,430,000.

8. Write an S above number 1 if 0.000000000000804 equals 8.04×10^{-13}.

9. Write a C above number 4 if 9.99×10^{-9} equals 0.000000000999.

10. Write an E above number 6 if 5.4286×10^{10} equals 54,286,000,000.

11. Write an N above number 4 if 1,700,000,000 equals 1.7×10^9.

12. Write an A above number 1 if 0.00000000003333 equals 3.33×10^{11}.

13. Write a T above number 5 if 90,420,000,000,000 equals 90.42×10^{13}.

14. Write an R above number 7 if 88.1×10^{-7} equals 0.000000881.

15. Write an I above number 3 if 6.05×10^{-8} equals 605,000,000.

16. Write an L above number 7 if 0.0000000000000000123 equals 1.23×10^{-17}.

17. Write a T above number 3 if 9,203,000,000,000,000,000, equals 92.03×10^{18}.

18. Write a U above number 3 if 8.541×10^{11} equals 854,100,000,000.

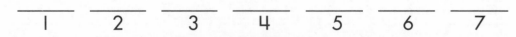

___ ___ ___ ___ ___ ___ ___
 1   2   3   4   5   6   7

                                       0-7424-1723-9 *Math*

Fractions as Repeating Decimals

Who was the first United States President
to throw out a baseball at a baseball game?

▶ Cross out the letters at the bottom of the page
if the fractions they represent have been incorrectly
written as repeating decimals.

A. $3\frac{5}{9} = 3.\overline{5}$

B. $\frac{10}{11} = 0.\overline{909}$

C. $\frac{16}{27} = .5\overline{92}$

D. $\frac{1}{22} = 0.0\overline{45}$

E. $\frac{21}{45} = 0.\overline{46}$

F. $8\frac{27}{33} = 8.\overline{81}$

G. $\frac{8}{45} = 0.1\overline{7}$

H. $\frac{7}{66} = 0.1\overline{06}$

I. $\frac{25}{54} = 0.4\overline{629}$

J. $4\frac{8}{15} = 4.5\overline{3}$

K. $\frac{17}{24} = 0.\overline{7083}$

L. $\frac{7}{33} = 0.\overline{21}$

M. $\frac{11}{18} = 0.6\overline{1}$

N. $3\frac{16}{99} = 3.1\overline{91}$

O. $3\frac{1}{6} = 3.1\overline{6}$

P. $\frac{15}{36} = 0.41\overline{6}$

Q. $4\frac{2}{3} = 0.\overline{6}$

R. $1\frac{8}{55} = 1.1\overline{45}$

S. $\frac{9}{74} = 0.12\overline{162}$

T. $\frac{47}{48} = 0.9791\overline{6}$

W. $\frac{7}{84} = 0.083\overline{3}$

W	B	Q	N	I	C	K	L	N	L	I	E	A	B	M	S
G	H	J	E	J	N	O	G	W	Q	A	P	R	J	K	D
S	G	K	T	B	E	C	A	N	F	E	C	C	P	T	S

0-7424-1723-9 *Math*

Percents, Decimals, and Fractions

Percent (%) means "per hundred." It is a ratio that compares a number to 100. It is the number of hundredths.

Fraction to Decimal	**Decimal to Fraction**
The fraction bar means divide.	Write the numeral as a fraction and reduce.

Fraction to Decimal
The fraction bar means divide.

$$\frac{3}{5} = 3 \div 5$$

$$\begin{array}{r} 0.6 \\ 5\overline{)3.0} \\ \underline{3\ 0} \\ 0 \end{array}$$

Decimal to Fraction
Write the numeral as a fraction and reduce.

0.35 = thirty-five hundredths =
$$\frac{35}{100} = \frac{7}{20}$$
0.015 = fifteen thousandths =
$$\frac{15}{1,000} = \frac{3}{200}$$

Percent to Decimal
Move the decimal two places to the left.

$$42\% = 0.42$$

$$1.87\% = 0.0187$$

Decimal to Percent
Move the decimal two places to the right.

$$0.08 = 8\%$$

$$0.73 = 73\%$$

▶ Complete the table.

	Percent	Decimal	Fraction
1.	50%		
2.		0.8	
3.			$\frac{1}{3}$
4.	$16\frac{2}{3}\%$		
5.		0.02	
6.			$\frac{1}{8}$
7.	$2\frac{1}{2}\%$		
8.		0.725	
9.			$\frac{2}{5}$

Mental Math: Calculating Tips

People often tip 15% for service in a restaurant. 15% = 10% + 5%.
To calculate 15% of a bill, move the decimal point one place to the left (10%) and add half that amount (5%).

$18 bill			$28.40 bill		
1.80	+ 0.90	= $2.70 tip	2.84	+ 1.42	= $4.26 tip
(10%)	($\frac{1}{2}$ of 1.80)		(10%)	($\frac{1}{2}$ of 2.85)	

▶ Use the shortcut to calculate 15% of each amount.

1. $9.00 _____ + _____ = _____

2. $32.60 _____ + _____ = _____

3. $48.00 _____ + _____ = _____

4. $72.60 _____ + _____ = _____

5. $120.00 _____ + _____ = _____

6. $250.00 _____ + _____ = _____

7. Explain how you could use a similar shortcut to calculate a 20% tip.

_____

_____

8. Explain how you could use a similar shortcut to calculate the discount on a 35% off sale.

_____

_____

Ratios as Percents

▶ Write the letter of the correct percent next to each ratio.

___ 1. $\frac{9}{16}$

___ 2. $111 : 250$

___ 3. $33 : 80$

___ 4. $\frac{14}{25}$

___ 5. $\frac{471}{500}$

___ 6. $7 : 8$

___ 7. $\frac{21}{32}$

___ 8. $4 : 5$

___ 9. $3 : 10$

___ 10. $321 : 400$

___ 11. $\frac{1}{4}$

___ 12. $\frac{191}{200}$

___ 13. $\frac{17}{20}$

___ 14. $29 : 40$

___ 15. $63 : 100$

___ 16. $\frac{99}{125}$

A. 56%

B. 65.625%

C. 44.4%

D. 95.5%

E. 87.5%

F. 85%

G. 80.25%

H. 63%

I. 41.25%

J. 80%

K. 56.25%

L. 94.2%

M. 25%

N. 72.5%

O. 79.2%

P. 30%

BEFORE

AFTER

Ratios in Context

A **ratio** is a size comparison of two numbers based on division.

There are twice as many boys as there are girls. If there are six boys, then how many girls are there?

Ratio of boys to girls: 2:1 (two to one)
Since there are twice as many boys as girls, divide the number of boys (6) by 2 to get the number of girls (3).

▶ Answer the questions.

1. A scale drawing shows the plans for a barn in a 1:48 ratio. On the plan, a wall of the barn is 2 feet in length. How long will the actual wall be?

2. A dessert recipe calls for 3 cups of flour and 1 cup of sugar. It serves 4 people. If the recipe must be altered to serve 12 people, how many cups of flour will be needed?

3. A restaurant has reserved seats for smokers and non-smokers in a 1:12 ratio. If there are only 10 seats for smokers, how many are reserved for non-smokers?

4. The ratio of people viewing comedy movies as compared to action movies is 5:3. If 200 people watch comedies, how many watch action movies?

5. A car model has a 1:36 scale. If a piece on the model is exactly one inch in length, how many feet would the actual piece be?

6. There are 240 patients in a hospital with health insurance, while 60 patients are without health insurance. Write a simplified ratio to express the number of insured patients to the number without insurance.

Finding Percentages

▶ Help Jerome get to the concert by connecting the tickets whose answers are 0.8%, 98%, 0.2%, 115%, 220%, and 18%.

A. What percent of 96 is 17.28?

B. 23 is what percent of 20?

C. What percent of 40 is 14?

D. 5.5 is what percent of 110?

E. What percent of 1,000 is 2?

F. 2.8 is what percent of 20?

G. 66 is what percent of 30?

H. What percent of 99 is 0.792?

I. What percent of 90 is 8.1?

J. 122.5 is what percent of 125?

K. 62.5 is what percent of 250?

L. 71.04 is what percent of 444?

Finding the Total Number

▶ Write the word form of the answers in the puzzle. Hint: Hyphens take up their own square.

ACROSS

3. 45% of what number is 8.1?

6. 3 is 4% of what number?

8. 40% of what number is 34?

9. 14 is 28% of what number?

12. 225% of what number is 81?

13. 9 is 15% of what number?

14. 111% of what number is 33.3?

DOWN

1. 7.8 is 65% of what number?

2. 2% of what number is 0.14?

4. 15.4 is 70% of what number?

5. 12% of what number is .6?

7. 80.51 is 97% of what number?

9. 165% of what number is 79.2?

10. 66 is 120% of what number?

11. 18% of what number is 16.56?

Percents and Proportions

What did Jack Broughton of Great Britain invent?

▶ Write the problem letter above its solution. Some answers will not be found in the puzzle.

H. What number is 18% of 250?

I. 72 is what percent of 60?

E. 5% of what number is 2?

O. What percent of 80 is 156?

E. What number is 53% of 300?

L. 25% of what number is 65?

E. 16 is what percent of 80?

L. What percent of 150 is 24?

U. What number is 75% of 20?

N. What percent of 20 is 22?

O. 15 is what percent of 500?

T. 800% of what number is 168?

B. What number is 40% of 15?

G. What percent of 400 is 820?

S. 70% of what number is 63?

V. What number is 340% of 5?

G. 36 is what percent of 150?

R. What percent of 50 is 4?

X. 25% of what number is 22?

___ ___ ___ ___ ___ ___ ___ ___ ___
21   45   20   6   195   88   120 110   24

___ ___ ___ ___ ___
205   16   3   17   159

Percent Increase and Decrease

▶ Match the percent increase or decrease to its correct answer.

_____ **1.** What is the percent increase from 40 to 64?

_____ **2.** What is the percent decrease from 50 to 3?

_____ **3.** What is 181 increased by 23%?

_____ **4.** What is 6 decreased by 62%?

_____ **5.** What is the percent increase from 25 to 95?

_____ **6.** What is 199 decreased by 9%?

_____ **7.** What is 15 increased by 68%?

_____ **8.** What is the percent decrease from 64 to 20?

_____ **9.** What is the percent increase form 60 to 102?

_____ **10.** What is 78 decreased by 5%?

_____ **11.** What is 87 increased by 45%?

_____ **12.** What is the percent decrease form 80 to 35?

A. 68.75%

B. 25.2

C. 2.28

D. 380%

E. 60%

F. 222.63

G. 56.25%

H. 94%

I. 181.09

J. 126.15

K. 74.1

L. 70%

0-7424-1723-9 *Math*

Name _____ Date _____

Simple Interest

Who said, "I shall return"?

▶ Find the simple interest. Write each letter above its answer. Round to the nearest cent.

	Principal	Yearly Interest Rate	Years
A.	$398.75	18%	13.5
L.	$420.10	$12\frac{1}{8}$%	19
H.	$875.00	$6\frac{3}{4}$%	8.75
R.	$1,342.38	11.6%	0.5
U.	$2,134.77	9%	5
A.	$986.50	6.8125%	2.25
A.	$880.25	22%	4.083
E.	$699.99	7%	18
L.	$3,000.00	$10\frac{7}{8}$%	1.25
U.	$719.30	16.05%	3.917
A.	$566.78	13%	8
R.	$410.50	$19\frac{1}{2}$%	0.75
R.	$315.00	28%	42
E.	$600.00	$8\frac{5}{8}$%	7.417
O.	$443.62	23%	13
T.	$1,050.00	16%	3
S.	$812.20	17.35%	1.67
N.	$5,000.00	18.15%	0.25
C.	$113.17	$25\frac{1}{4}$%	28
D.	$386.49	20%	4
G.	$78.00	19.3%	5.25
M.	$2,046.00	$7\frac{1}{4}$%	0.67
G.	$525.15	11%	39

$79.03 $881.99 $226.88 $383.83 $77.86 $589.45 $407.81

$309.19 $1,326.42 $960.65 $2,252.89 $967.81 $790.69 $235.33

$99.38 $151.21 $800.11 $968.96 $3,704.40 $504 $516.80 $452.21 $60.04

Compound Interest

Who has sold more records in more languages than any other musical artist in history?

▶ Find the total amount after the given number of years. Write the letter from the "amount" column above its answer. Round to the nearest cent. Hint: $A = P(1 + \frac{r}{n})^{nt}$, where A = amount, P = principal, r = rate, n = compounded, and t = years.

Principal	Interest Rate	Compounded	Time	Amount
$3,000.00	18%	annually	2 years	G
$450.00	$9\frac{1}{4}$%	monthly	4 years	A
$900.00	11.6%	semiannually	18 years	S
$1,500.00	24%	quarterly	9 years	L
$875.00	15%	annually	5 years	I
$5,000	$8\frac{3}{8}$%	semiannually	2 years	U
$1,650.00	6%	quarterly	1 year	E
$75.00	$17\frac{1}{2}$%	semiannually	18 years	I
$1,925.00	13.2%	annually	3 years	O
$2,000.00	$3\frac{5}{8}$%	monthly	5 years	L
$650.00	2%	quarterly	6 years	S
$300.00	14.4%	annually	4 years	J
$6,500.00	$10\frac{1}{8}$%	semiannually	2 years	I

‾‾‾‾‾ ‾‾‾‾‾ ‾‾‾‾‾ ‾‾‾‾‾ ‾‾‾‾‾
$513.84 $5,891.59 $2,396.77 $1,759.94 $2,792.35

‾‾‾‾‾ ‾‾‾‾‾ ‾‾‾‾‾ ‾‾‾‾‾ ‾‾‾‾‾ ‾‾‾‾‾ ‾‾‾‾‾ ‾‾‾‾‾
$7,919.62 $4,177.20 $12,220.88 $1,751.25 $732.65 $1,536.44. $650.56 $6,850.57

Name _____ Date _____

Commission

Most presidents have careers before being elected. What was one of Woodrow Wilson's occupations besides being President of the United States?

TWEET!

► Cross out the letter each time it appears at the bottom of the page if the commission was figured incorrectly. Round to the nearest cent.

Rate of Commission	Total Sales	Commission	Rate of Commission	Total Sales	Commission
A. 12.6%	$850.00	$107.10	N. 7%	$6,428.00	$450.00
B. 15%	$915.26	$137.29	O. 9.3%	$515.25	$47.92
C. $9\frac{1}{4}$%	$3,546.95	$328.09	P. $12\frac{1}{2}$%	$489.99	$51.25
D. 13.1%	$717.00	$93.93	Q. 18%	$200.75	$36.15
E. 21%	$2,540.20	$533.44	R. $29\frac{1}{4}$%	$907.00	$265.20
F. 28%	$632.00	$176.96	S. 30%	$811.35	$343.41
G. 3%	$914.88	$27.45	T. 26%	$1,346.00	$349.96
H. 5.5%	$1,005.00	$55.28	U. $4\frac{7}{8}$%	$4,320.75	$220.64
I. 8.8%	$5,693.00	$400.98	V. 30%	$516.00	$154.00
J. 6%	$489.16	$29.34	W. 2%	$981.30	$19.53
K. 16.95%	$225.25	$38.17	X. 48%	$562.89	$271.19
L. $8\frac{3}{4}$%	$900.00	$78.75	Y. 1.1%	$3,110.00	$33.21
M. $7\frac{3}{8}$%	$485.50	$35.80	Z. 5.5%	$876.25	$48.20

M I R H S P E P N J V N W K

J N C K O A U C M H Y E D N

C O Q W M L I U L S E R G E

P F I O X M O T B Z A L S L

0-7424-1723-9 *Math*

Percents in Context

▶ Solve the problems below.

1. Warren is going to use the $26,200 in his savings account to buy a new car. The car he plans to buy costs $24,244.33 plus sales tax, which is $4\frac{1}{4}$%. How much money will Warren have in his account after buying the car and paying the sales tax?

2. Last year, Stephanie was paid a base salary of $12,000 per year plus a commission of 3% on the total dollar value of her sales. She sold $1,120,000 worth of company products. How much did she make?

3. This year, Stephanie's new commission rate will be cut to 2.8%, but her base salary will be raised to $14,000 per year. Should Stephanie be concerned? What would the difference in her salary have been if this plan had been in place last year?

4. A painting by a famous Impressionist sold through an auction house where the sale price is not publicly disclosed. The auction house works on a commission rate of 10%. They earned a commission of $400,000 on this painting. What was the price of the painting?

Name _____

Date _____

Powers and Roots

▲ Tony, the trivia buff, sent this message in code by telegram so nobody but mathematic scholars could figure it out. Use the decoder box below to crack the code and learn this interesting fact.

TELEGRAM

$\sqrt[3]{27}$ 5^4 $\sqrt[5]{32}$ STOP 3^2 $\sqrt{625}$ STOP 3^2 $\sqrt[3]{1000}$ 3^4 $\sqrt[7]{128}$ $\sqrt[3]{125}$ $\sqrt[5]{243}$ STOP

4^4 $\sqrt[3]{8}$ 4^2 5^2 16^2 $\sqrt[3]{216}$ STOP 25^2 $\sqrt{36}$ $\sqrt{4}$ $\sqrt{256}$ 2^4 $\sqrt{169}$ 15^2 -

$\sqrt{50,625}$ $\sqrt[3]{512}$ $\sqrt{100}$ 9^2 STOP $\sqrt[5]{243}$ $\sqrt{9}$ $\sqrt[4]{256}$ 2^2 4^2

$\sqrt{81}$ $\sqrt[3]{64}$ $\sqrt{25}$ $\sqrt[4]{81}$ $\sqrt{4}$ $\sqrt{36}$ STOP $\sqrt[4]{625}$ 2^3 $\sqrt{121}$ $\sqrt[3]{27}$ $\sqrt[3]{8000}$ -

12^2 $\sqrt{64}$ 11^2 $\sqrt[4]{16}$ STOP $\sqrt{400}$ $\sqrt[6]{64}$ 2^8 $\sqrt[3]{125}$ STOP

Decoder Box

A = 4	**G** = 81	**M** = 170	**S** = 5
B = 12	**H** = 625	**N** = 10	**T** = 3
C = 16	**I** = 8	**O** = 25	**U** = 13
D = 6	**J** = 254	**P** = 225	**V** = 121
E = 2	**K** = 7	**Q** = 211	**W** = 169
F = 144	**L** = 9	**R** = 256	**X** = 11
			Y = 20
			Z = 196

Order of Operations

Mathematicians have agreed on a standard order of operations. The following phrase may help you remember the order. Each letter in the phrase stands for a mathematical operation.

Please

Excuse

My

Dear

Aunt

Sally

Parentheses

Exponents
(includes roots)

Multiplication

Division

Addition

Subtraction

▶ Follow the order of operations to solve the problems below. You may need to use more than one step to get the final solution.

1. $35 + 50 + \dfrac{25}{5} \times 5 - (8 + 11)$

2. $(^-16 + 20)^2 + 6 \div (6 + 2) + \sqrt{49}$

3. $3 + 2^3 (4 + 9 \div 3)$

4. $5 - 48 \div (12 + 4) - \sqrt{16}$

5. $\dfrac{1}{2} (^-12 - 8) + \sqrt{(16 + 9)}$

6. $\sqrt[3]{64} \div (4 \times 5 - 36 \div 2) + {}^-3$

7. $\dfrac{1}{4} [^-4(3 - 12) - 20]$

8. $\sqrt[3]{5(20 - 2) + \dfrac{30}{2} + 6 \times 3 + 2}$

9. $15 - 8 \times 2 + 11 + 5^2 \times 2$

10. $2^3 - \sqrt[3]{^-19 + 2 + (1 + 4)^2}$

0-7424-1723-9 *Math*

Factorials

What is the capital of the U.S. Virgin Islands?

▶ Find the value. Write the corresponding letter above that value.

T. $(4!)(5!)$ **E.** $6! + 3!$ **I.** $12! \div 10!$ **M.** $\dfrac{14!}{10!}$ **R.** $\left(\dfrac{12}{3}\right)!$

H. $(6 - 3)!$ **O.** $7!$ **E.** $8! - 4!$ **A.** $\dfrac{11!}{(15 - 8)!}$ **L.** $\dfrac{5!}{4!}$

A. $\dfrac{9!}{3!}$ **T.** $2!$ **A.** $(23 - 14)!$ **L.** $\dfrac{(6!)(4!)}{4!}$ **C.** $\dfrac{(8!)(3!)}{5!}$

$\overline{\text{2,016}}$ $\overline{\text{6}}$ $\overline{\text{362,880}}$ $\overline{\text{24}}$ $\overline{\text{720}}$ $\overline{\text{5,040}}$ $\overline{\text{2,880}}$ $\overline{\text{2}}$ $\overline{\text{726}}$

$\overline{\text{7,920}}$ $\overline{\text{24,024}}$ $\overline{\text{60,480}}$ $\overline{\text{5}}$ $\overline{\text{132}}$ $\overline{\text{40,296}}$

Absolute Value

Which invention, created in 1969, revolutionized home entertainment?

▶ Simplify the following absolute value expressions. Write the letter that corresponds to the problem above the answer at the bottom of the page.

C. $|26 - 31|$ **E.** $|^-5 \times 3|$

A. $|^-8| \times |7|$ **V.** $|30| \div |^-5|$ **T.** $|32 + {}^-39|$

I. $|^-81 \div 9|$ **S.** $|^-7| \times |^-3|$ **O.** $|^-18| - |21|$

E. $|^-50| \div {}^-5$ **E.** $^-16 + |^-4|$ **T.** $|^-54 \div 3|$

A. $|-13 + 3|$ **D.** $|8 \times {}^-3|$ **T.** $|^-64| - 66$

S. $^-6 \times |-3|$ **P.** $|^-49| + {}^-7$ **E.** $|^-63| \div |21|$

6	9	24	15	-3	7	56	42	3

5	10	⁻18	21	⁻10	18	⁻2	⁻12

Find the Number

► Use the clues to find the number.

1. There are four different digits.
The hundreds digit is double the even thousands digit.
The sum of the digits is 14.
The ones digit is one more than the hundreds digit.

—— —— —— ——

2. There are four different digits.
The thousands digit (the only prime) is one less than the hundreds digit.
The number formed by adding the tens and ones is double the hundreds digit.
The ones digit is one less than the thousands digit.

—— —— —— ——

3. There are four different digits.
The ones digit is the largest digit and the square of the tens digit.
The hundreds digit is greater than the thousands digit.
The sum of the digits is 15.

—— —— —— ——

4. There are four different digits.
The hundreds digit is half the thousands digit.
The ones digit is 2 less than the sum of the thousands and hundreds digits.
The sum of the digits is 15.

—— —— —— ——

5. There are four different digits.
There are no zeros.
The tenths digit is double the ones digit.
The hundredths digit is one less than the tenths digit.
The sum of the digits is 14.

—— —— . —— ——

6. There are four different digits.
There are no zeros or twos.
The tens digit is a multiple of 2, the ones digit is a multiple of 3, the tenths digit is a multiple of 4, and the hundredths digit is a multiple of 5.
The sum of the digits is 18.

—— —— . —— ——

Magic Square

A **Magic Square** is a square arrangement of numbers in which the sum of the numbers in each row, column, and diagonal is the same.

▶ Below are the pieces of a Magic Square. Assemble the pieces into a 4-by-4 Magic Square.

7
2

10	3
26	

11
5
4

25	1	12

8	24

	27
6	9

Number Systems

▶ Use the terms **integers, irrationals, mixed numbers, proper fractions, whole numbers,** and **reals.**

1. Fill in the organizational chart to show the relationships between the types of numbers.

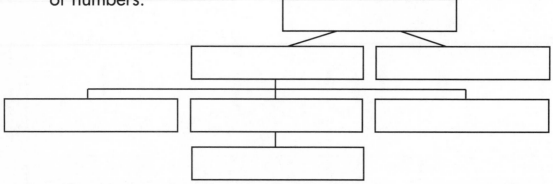

2. Label the regions of the Venn diagram with the terms given above.

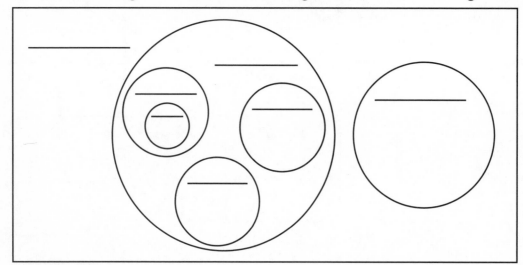

3. Place each of the following numbers in the most appropriate region of the Venn diagram.

$\dfrac{2}{3}$ $\sqrt{19}$ -24 $4\dfrac{1}{3}$ 0 $\sqrt{9}$

5.5 $\dfrac{1}{5}$ 7   π   -3 $\sqrt{26}$

Commutative Property

Addition and multiplication are **commutative** operations because $a + b = b + a$ and $ab = ba$.

If A::B = 2A − B, is :: commutative? In other words, does A::B = B::A?
(:: represents an operation)

$$A::B = 2A - B$$

$$4::5 = 2(4) - 5 \qquad\qquad 5::4 = 2(5) - 4$$
$$= 8 - 5 \qquad\qquad\qquad = 10 - 4$$
$$= 3 \qquad\qquad\qquad\qquad = 6$$

Solution: Since 3 ≠ 6, the operation :: is not commutative.

▶ Determine if the defined operation is commutative. Justify your answer by showing examples or explaining your reasoning.

1. If A ➡ B = 2(A + B),
does A ➡ B = B ➡ A?

_____

_____

2. If A ♦ B = 2A + B,
does A ♦ B = B ♦ A?

_____

_____

3. If A ■ B = $B^2 + A^2$,
does A ■ B = B ■ A?

_____

_____

4. If A ▲ B = AB + BA,
does A ▲ B = B ▲ A?

_____

_____

5. If A ★ B = $A^2 - B$,
does A ★ B = B ★ A?

_____

_____

6. If A ⊕ = A^B,
does A ⊕ B = B ⊕ A?

_____

_____

Associative and Distributive Properties

The **associative property** uses only one operation (such as addition).
The **distributive property** involves two different operations (such as multiplication and addition) at the same time.

Associative Property

$a + (b + c) = (a + b) + c$
$2 + (3 + 5) = (2 + 3) + 5$

$a(bc) = (ab)c$
$2 \times (3 \times 5) = (2 \times 3) \times 5$

Distributive Property

$a(b + c) = ab + ac$
$2(3 + 5) = 2 \times 3 + 2 \times 5$

$(b - c)a = ba - ca$
$(6 - 2)4 = 6 \times 4 - 2 \times 4$

▶ Examine each equation. If the equation is correct, write the property (*associative* or *distributive*) on the line. If the equation is incorrect, write *false* on the line.

1. $2(3n) = (2 \times 3)n$ _____

2. $2(3 + n) = (2 + 3) \times (2 + n)$ _____

3. $4 + (3 + k) = (4 \times 3) \times k$ _____

4. $6(n + 2) = 6n + 12$ _____

5. $18 + (3 \times 2) = (18 + 3) \times 2$ _____

6. $(4 + t) + 5 = 4 + (t + 5)$ _____

7. $4p + 28 = 4(p + 7)$ _____

8. $8(m + 1) = 8m$ _____

9. $7 (4s) = (7 \times 4)s$ _____

▶ Use the associative and distributive properties to simplify the expressions below. Show your steps.

10. $6(2n) + 3(r + 2)$ **11.** $(5t + 2u) + 3u + 4(v - 2)$ **12.** $8p + (4p + t) + 2(t + 3)$

Patterns

▶ Find the missing numbers in each series. Describe the pattern algebraically.

1. 3, 8, 15, 20, _____ , 32, 39, _____ , 51, 56

Pattern _____

2. 100, 120, 140, 160, 180, _____ , _____ , _____

Pattern _____

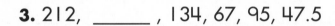

3. 212, _____ , 134, 67, 95, 47.5

Pattern _____

4. 3, 9, 81, _____

Pattern _____

5. 1, 5, 25, 125, _____ , _____

Pattern _____

▶ Solve for each missing part of the pattern. Then, write a short description of each pattern.

6. ⁻6, ⁻5, ⁻3, 0, 4, _____ , _____ , _____

7. X, U, R, _____ , _____ , I, F, C

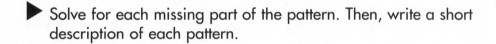

8. △△▢▢△△△▢▢△△▢▢

Series

▶ Find the pattern. Complete the tables.

1.

1	2	3	4	5	10	N
1	4	9	16	25		

2.

1	2	3	4	5	10	N
0.5	1	1.5	2	2.5		

3.

1	2	3	4	5	10	N
1	8	27	64	125		

4.

1	2	3	4	5	10	N
9	8	7	6	5		

5.

1	2	3	4	5	10	N
2	4	8	16	32		

▶ Make up your own pattern:

6.

1	2	3	4	5	10	N

0-7424-1723-9 Math

Graphs and Relationships

▶ Which graph most likely shows the following?

A. relationship between centimeters and inches
B. pairs of possible positive integer factors of 24
C. cost of postage compared to weight
D. resale value of a car based on its age
E. growth of virus over time
F. time awake versus time asleep

1. _____

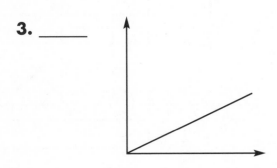

2. _____

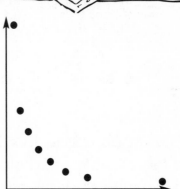

3. _____

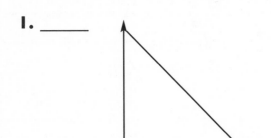

4. _____

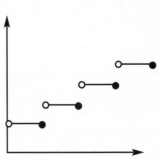

5. _____

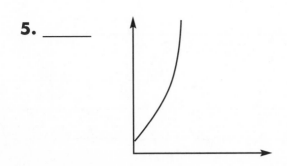

6. _____

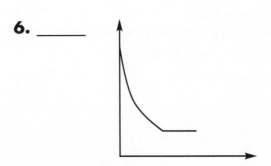

Graphs and Rates of Change

1. Keisha traveled by car from her house to visit her cousin. The graph represents her trip. Match the intervals with what might have happened.

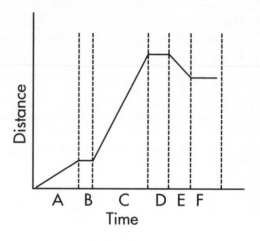

_____**1.** drives on a neighborhood street

_____**2.** stops at a one-minute stop light

_____**3.** drives on a freeway

_____**4.** drives into a parking spot

_____**5.** stops in parking spot

_____**6.** stops briefly at a stop sign

2. The graph relates to a boy, his dog, and a tub of water. Explain what might have happened during each interval.

A. _____

B. _____

C. _____

D. _____

E. _____

F. _____

G. _____

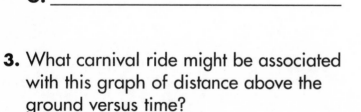

3. What carnival ride might be associated with this graph of distance above the ground versus time?

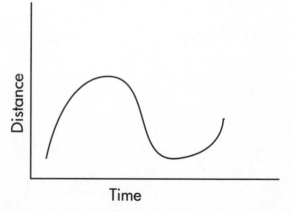

Solving by Substitution

> How do you catch a unique rabbit?

▶ Evaluate the expressions using $n = 3$, $c = 4$, and $x = 5$. Write the letter above its answer.

U. x^2 **E.** $\dfrac{nc}{6}$ **N.** $5c - 7n$ **H.** $\dfrac{77}{n + c}$

I. $8(n - x)$ **I.** $6(n + c)$ **U.** $2cx$ **P.** n^3

U. $\dfrac{29 - n^2}{x}$ **N.** $c^2 + x$ **M.** $10n \div 2x$ **O.** $^-x(7 + c)$

Q. $\dfrac{n^2 - x^2}{c}$

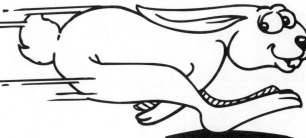

$\overline{}$ $\overline{}$ $\overline{}$ $\overline{}$ $\overline{}$ $\overline{}$
40   21   42   ⁻4   4   2

$\overline{}$ $\overline{}$ $\overline{}$ $\overline{}$ $\overline{}$ $\overline{}$ $\overline{}$
25   27   ⁻55   ⁻1   11   ⁻16   3

> How do you catch a tame rabbit?

▶ Follow the directions above using $y = ^-6$, $a = ^-5$, and $m = 2$.

A. $\dfrac{ya}{m}$ **A.** $m(y + a)$ **E.** $3y + 11$ **Y.** y^m

E. $8(a - y)$ **T.** $a^2 + 2y$ **H.** $\dfrac{-77}{y + a}$ **W.** $3m^4$

T. $\dfrac{-9am}{y}$ **M.** $\dfrac{120}{ya}$

$\overline{}$ $\overline{}$ $\overline{}$ $\overline{}$ $\overline{}$ $\overline{}$ $\overline{}$ $\overline{}$ $\overline{}$ $\overline{}$
⁻15   7   ⁻7   13   15   4   8   48   ⁻22   36

     0-7424-1723-9 *Math*

Name _____

Date _____

Equations: Checking Solutions

$39 - c = 12$ $c = 27$	$48 - c = -11$ $c = 59$	$\frac{a}{15} = 5$ $a = 75$	$5x + 15 = 40$ $x = 4$	$20x = -100$ $x = 5$
$36 = 12x$ $x = 3$	$\frac{x}{12} = 12$ $x = -144$	$y + {}^-12 = -19$ $y = -7$	$66 = 11x$ $x = -6$	$\frac{x}{13} = -11$ $c = -169$
$a - 10 = -2$ $a = 8$	$-13 + w = 5$ $w = 8$	$8a = -72$ $a = -9$	$\frac{n}{8} = 7$ $n = -56$	$16 + x = -8$ $x = 24$
$\frac{m}{9} = 7$ $m = 63$	$64 = 7c$ $c = -8$	$99 = 33b$ $b = 3$	$r - 17 = 26$ $r = 44$	$28 + m = 5$ $m = -33$
$7b = -70$ $b = -10$	$19 = 22 + n$ $n = -41$	$6x = 48$ $x = 8$	$\frac{c}{11} = -4$ $c = -44$	$\frac{b}{14} = 3$ $b = 84$
$x - 13 = 5$ $x = 18$	$8 = -15 + b$ $b = -7$	$7a = 49$ $a = -7$	$24 + w = -6$ $w = -30$	$52 = 4y$ $y = 12$
$26 = 4 + y$ $y = 22$	$x - 17 = 3$ $x = 14$	$\frac{m}{4} = 8$ $m = 38$	$y - 14 = -5$ $y = 9$	$5 = x - 8$ $x = 13$
$7b = -28$ $b = 4$	$\frac{x}{5} = 15$ $x = 65$	$29 - a = -14$ $a = 15$	$-11 = r - 40$ $r = -51$	$41 = -5 + c$ $c = 46$

0-7424-1723-9 *Math*

Name _____ Date _____ Algebra

Solving 1-Step Equations

At the Winter Olympics in 1998, the U.S. team won the first Olympic gold medal awarded for which sport?

▶ Solve these equations. Write the letter above its correct solution below.

H. $^-20 = x + 11$

E. $^-16 = 23 - x$

I. $^-7 = ^-10 + x$

K. $53 - x = 72$

E. $x - 27 = ^-4$

M. $12 = 6 - x$

N. $13 = ^-41 + x$

O. $^-16 = ^-25 - x$

O. $^-12x = ^-120$

C. $\dfrac{x}{25} = 3$

Y. $^-8 = \dfrac{x}{^-2}$

W. $^-36x = 4$

S. $49x = 7$

E. $^-5 = \dfrac{x}{11}$

C. $64x = 12$

$$\overline{}_{\frac{^-1}{9}} \quad \overline{}_{10} \quad \overline{}_{^-6} \quad \overline{}_{^-55} \quad \overline{}_{54} \; {}^, \quad \overline{}_{\frac{1}{7}} \qquad \overline{}_{3} \quad \overline{}_{75} \quad \overline{}_{23}$$

$$\overline{}_{^-31} \quad \overline{}_{^-9} \quad \overline{}_{\frac{3}{16}} \quad \overline{}_{^-19} \quad \overline{}_{39} \quad \overline{}_{16}$$

+ ◆ ⌐ ● x ◆ ÷ ▶ + ◢ ⌐ ● x ◆ ÷ ▶ + ◢ ⌐ ● x ◆ ÷ ▶

Solving Equations: Scrambled Steps

▶ In each problem, the steps for solving the equation are scrambled. Rewrite the steps in the correct order.

1. $2(x - 3) + 4x = 8 - x$

A. $7x - 6 = 8$

B. $2x - 6 + 4x = 8 - x$

C. $7x = 14$

D. $6x - 6 = 8 - x$

E. $x = 2$

$2(x - 3) + 4x = 8 - x$

_____

_____

_____

_____

_____

2. $5 - 3(x - 2) = 4(x + 1)$

A. $7 = 7x$

B. $11 - 3x = 4x + 4$

C. $1 = x$

D. $11 = 7x + 4$

E. $5 - 3x + 6 = 4x + 4$

$5 - 3(x - 2) = 4(x + 1)$

_____

_____

_____

_____

_____

3. $^-6x - 2(x + 1) = x + 7$

A. $^-2 = 9x + 7$

B. $^-1 = x$

C. $^-8x - 2 = x + 7$

D. $^-6x - 2x - 2 = x + 7$

E. $^-9 = 9x$

$^-6x - 2(x + 1) = x + 7$

_____

_____

_____

_____

_____

4. $3(2x - 1) = 7 + 2(x - 5)$

A. $6x - 3 = 2x - 3$

B. $6x - 3 = 7 + 2x - 10$

C. $4x = 0$

D. $x = 0$

E. $4x - 3 = ^-3$

$3(2x - 1) = 7 + 2(x - 5)$

_____

_____

_____

_____

_____

Equations Involving Two Operations

▶ Find the solutions to the equations. Show your work.

1. $\dfrac{x}{5} + 11 = 18$

2. $5r - 140 = {}^-15$

3. $\dfrac{n}{{}^-7} - 5 = 4$

4. $^-29 = 11p + 59$

5. $15 = 120 + 3b$

6. $38 - \dfrac{a}{11} = 34$

7. $^-111 + 2s = 9$

8. $^-5 = \dfrac{c}{8} - 12$

9. $8 - \dfrac{y}{15} = 12$

10. $86 = {}^-5m + 11$

11. $9 = 21 - \dfrac{c}{9}$

12. $110 + 2r = 20$

13. $7y + 90 = 6$

14. $20 - 4c = {}^-68$

15. $^-29 = \dfrac{x}{14} - 23$

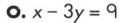

Functions: Checking Solutions

What animal, which can move 100-200 mph, is the world's fastest?

▶ Find the ordered pair that solves each of the following equations. Write the corresponding letter above each ordered pair.

I. $y = {}^-2x - 1$　　　　**A.** $4 - y = x$

G. $8 = x - y$　　　　**E.** $y = \dfrac{x}{2}$

O. $x - 3y = 9$　　　　**N.** $7 - x = y$

R. $2x + 3y = 9$　　　**L.** $x = {}^-y + 1$　　　**E.** $x + y = 3$

N. $y = 25 + 3x$　　　**E.** $12 = 5x + 4y$　　　**R.** ${}^-3x = {}^-y$

C. $2x = 14 + y$　　　**P.** $x = 17 - y$　　　**F.** $4y + 19 = x$

$\overline{\hspace{1em}}$ $\overline{\hspace{1em}}$ $\overline{\hspace{1em}}$ $\overline{\hspace{1em}}$ $\overline{\hspace{1em}}$ $\overline{\hspace{1em}}$ $\overline{\hspace{1em}}$ $\overline{\hspace{1em}}$ $\overline{\hspace{1em}}$
(12, 5)　(20, 10)　(7, ⁻21)　(4, ⁻2)　(11, 3)　(⁻3, 5)　(⁻6, 11)　(⁻5, 12)　(⁻5, 8)

$\overline{\hspace{1em}}$ $\overline{\hspace{1em}}$ $\overline{\hspace{1em}}$ $\overline{\hspace{1em}}$ $\overline{\hspace{1em}}$ $\overline{\hspace{1em}}$
(⁻5, ⁻6)　(7, ⁻3)　(4, ⁻3)　(20, 26)　(⁻6, ⁻5)　(⁻3, 16)

Coordinate Grids: Quadrants

The four regions of the plane determined by the x-axis and y-axis are called **quadrants**.

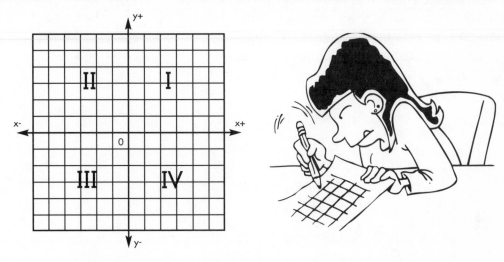

▶ Give the location by quadrant (I through IV), axis (x or y), or origin. There may be more than one answer.

1. ($^-$1, 5) _____   **2.** (2, 3) _____   **3.** (0, 0) _____

4. (4, 0) _____   **5.** (0, $^-$3) _____   **6.** ($^-$3, $^-$9) _____

7. ($x < 0, y > 0$) _____   **8.** ($x > 0$) _____   **9.** ($x = 0$) _____

10. ($y = 0$) _____   **11.** ($x \leq 0, y > 0$) _____   **12.** ($y < 0$) _____

▶ Write the quadrant(s) in which the graphs of these equations lie. There may be more than one answer.

13. $x = ^-3$ _____   **14.** $y = ^-5$ _____   **15.** $y = 7$ _____

16. $x = 9$ _____   **17.** $y = x^2$ _____   **18.** $y = x$ _____

19. $x = y^2$ _____   **20.** $y = ^-x$ _____

Slope Between Two Points

Slope is the ratio of rise/run and indicates the steepness of the graph of a line. The **rise** is the vertical change and the **run** is the horizontal change.

▶ Find the slope of each line.

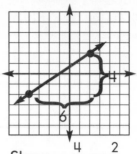

Slope = $\frac{4}{6}$ or $\frac{2}{3}$

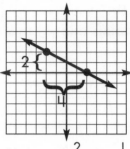

Slope = $-\frac{2}{4}$ or $-\frac{1}{2}$

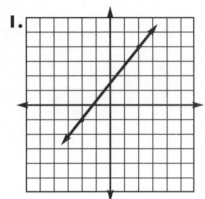

1.

2.

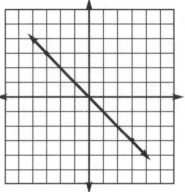

3.

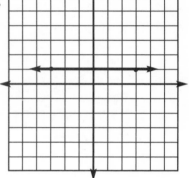

4. If a line rises from left to right, what can be said of the slope? _____

5. If a line falls from left to right, what can be said of the slope? _____

Slope can be determined from the coordinates of two points on the line.

(2, 3) and (4, 9)

$\frac{\text{rise}}{\text{run}} = \frac{9-3}{4-2} = \frac{6}{2} = 3$

(6, 1) and (⁻2, 4)

$\frac{\text{rise}}{\text{run}} = \frac{4-1}{⁻2-6} = -\frac{3}{8}$

▶ Find the slope of the line passing through the two points.

6. (0, 2) and (3, 4) **7.** (⁻1, 3) and (2, 1) **8.** (2, ⁻4) and (1, 1)

The Distance Formula

To find the distance between the 2 points (x_1, y_1) and (x_2, y_2), Use the formula.

$$D = \sqrt{(x_2 - x_1)^2 + (y_2 - y_1)^2}$$

Find the distance between $(^-3, 2)$ and $(1, ^-2)$.

$$D = \sqrt{(1 - ^-3)^2 + (^-2 - 2)^2}$$

$$= \sqrt{(4)^2 + (^-4)^2} = \sqrt{16 + 16}$$

$$= \sqrt{32} = \sqrt{2 \times 2 \times 2 \times 2 \times 2}$$

$$= 4\sqrt{2}$$

▶ Find the distance between each pair of points. Round to the nearest hundredth.

1. $(6, 4)$ and $(2, 1)$

2. $(^-2, ^-4)$ and $(3, 8)$

3. $(0, 0)$ and $(5, 10)$

4. $(^-5, 2)$ and $(7, ^-7)$

5. $(0, ^-8)$ and $(8, 7)$

6. $(^-2, 11)$ and $(4, 3)$

7. $(2, 1)$ and $(4, 0)$

8. $(6, 4)$ and $(6, ^-2)$

9. $(^-2, 2)$ and $(4, ^-1)$

10. $(^-3, ^-5)$ and $(2, 5)$

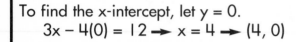

Linear Equations: Finding Intercepts

When an equation is in **a**x + **b**y = **c** form, use the x-intercept and the y-intercept to graph the line.

Graph 3x − 4y = 12.

To find the x-intercept, let y = 0.
　3x − 4(0) = 12 ➡ x = 4 ➡ (4, 0)

To find the y-intercept, let x = 0.
　3(0) − 4y = 12 ➡ y = ⁻3 ➡ (0, ⁻3)

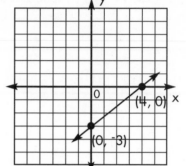

▶ For each equation find the intercepts, plot the points, and draw the line.

1. 2x + 3y = 6

x	y
0	
	0

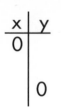
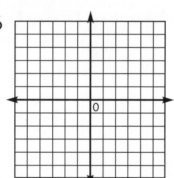

2. 2x − 5y = ⁻10

x	y
0	
	0

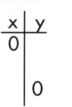
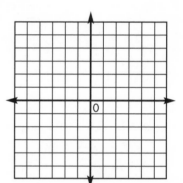

3. x − 5y = 5

x	y

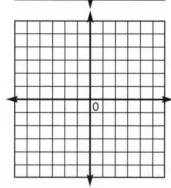

4. x − y = ⁻3

x	y

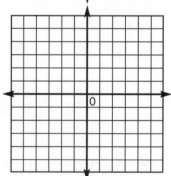

5. 2x + ½ y = ⁻2

x	y

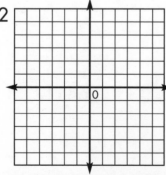

6. x + ⅓ y = 1

x	y

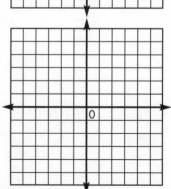

Linear Equations: Slope-Intercept Form

The slope and y-intercept can be used to draw the graph of an equation.

1. Write the equation in $y = \mathbf{m}x + \mathbf{b}$ form; $\mathbf{m}$ is the slope and $(o, \mathbf{b})$ is the y-intercept.

2. Plot $\mathbf{m}$ as a ratio (change in y/change in x).

3. Write $(0, \mathbf{b})$.

4. Start at $(0, \mathbf{b})$. Count up for positive change in y or down for negative change in y. Count over for the change in x—to the right if positive, to the left if negative.

5. Plot the point and draw the line.

$x + 3y = 6$

1. $y = \frac{-x}{3} + 2$

2. Plot $\mathbf{b} = (0, 2)$

3. $\mathbf{m} = -\frac{1}{3}$

4. Count down 1 and to the right 3.

5. Plot the point and draw the line.

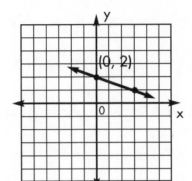

▶ Use the slope-intercept form to graph each equation.

1. $y = 2x - 1$

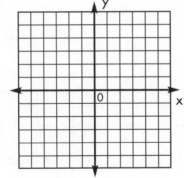

2. $y + x = 1$

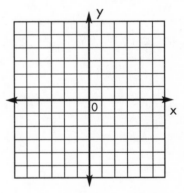

3. $2y = x - 4$

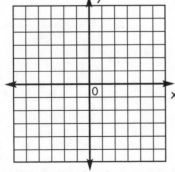

4. $2y = 3x + 6$

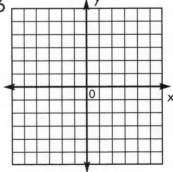

Linear Equations: Graphs

► In the linear equation $y = \mathbf{m}x + \mathbf{b}$, $\mathbf{m}$ is the slope of the line and $\mathbf{b}$ is the y-intercept. Match each clue to its correct equation and graph.

Clue: Equation: Graph:

1. Slope is greater than 3. Y-intercept is negative.   _____ _____

2. Slope is a negative integer. Y-intercept is above the *x*-axis. _____ _____

3. Slope is positive. Y-intercept is the origin.   _____ _____

4. Slope is less than ⁻3. Y-intercept is negative.   _____ _____

5. Slope is 0. Y-intercept is even.   _____ _____

6. Slope is between 0 and 1. Y-intercept is less than 0.   _____ _____

7. Slope is between ⁻1 and 0. Y-intercept is prime.   _____ _____

8. Slope is ⁻1. Y-intercept is 0.   _____ _____

Equations   Graphs

A. $y = 2x$

B. $y = 2$

C. $y = -\frac{1}{2}x + 3$

D. $y = {}^-4x - 3$

E. $y = 4x - 3$

F. $y = \frac{1}{2}x - 3$

G. $y = {}^-x$

H. $y = {}^-3x + 2$

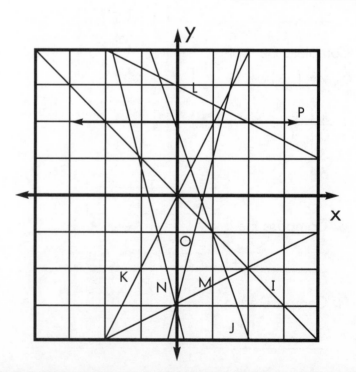

Parallel and Perpendicular Lines

Parallel lines never intersect. **Perpendicular** lines meet at a right angle.

▶ Complete the tables and graph the equations.

1. $y = 3x - 4$

x	y
0	⁻4
1	
2	

2. $y = 3x - 1$

x	y
0	⁻1
1	
2	

3. $y = x - 4$

x	y
0	⁻4
1	
2	

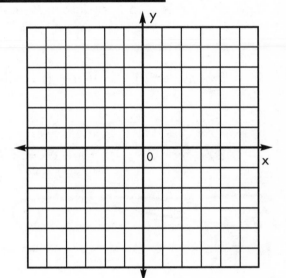

4. What do equations 1 and 2 have in common? How does this make the graphs look?

_____

_____

5. What do the equations 1 and 3 have in common? How does this make the graphs look?

_____

_____

▶ Complete the tables and graph the equations.

6. $y = (\frac{2}{3})x + 1$ **7.** $y = (-\frac{3}{2})x + 1$

x	y
0	1
3	
6	

x	y
0	1
2	
4	

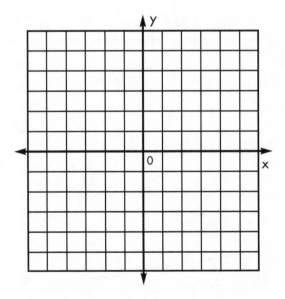

8. Compare the graphs for equations 6 and 7.

_____

9. Compare equations 6 and 7.

_____

Systems of Equations

▶ Poor Pauline the Pirate has a map to buried treasure but doesn't understand algebra. To help her, first find the point that is a solution to the system of equations. Then, connect the points on the map in order and draw the path to the hidden treasure.

1. $x = {}^-y$
$2x - 3y = {}^-35$

2. $2x = {}^-y$
$7x - 2y = {}^-44$

3. ${}^-5x = y$
$2x + y = 3$

4. $y = 2x$
${}^-3x + 10y = 34$

5. $x = 7y$
$4x - 9y = 19$

6. $3y = {}^-x$
$8y + 3x = 3$

7. ${}^-y = 3x$
$5y - 6x = {}^-63$

8. $y = 5x$
$7x - 2y = 6$

9. $y = 2x$
$11x - 6y = 3$

10. $x = 2y$
${}^-3y + 2x = {}^-5$

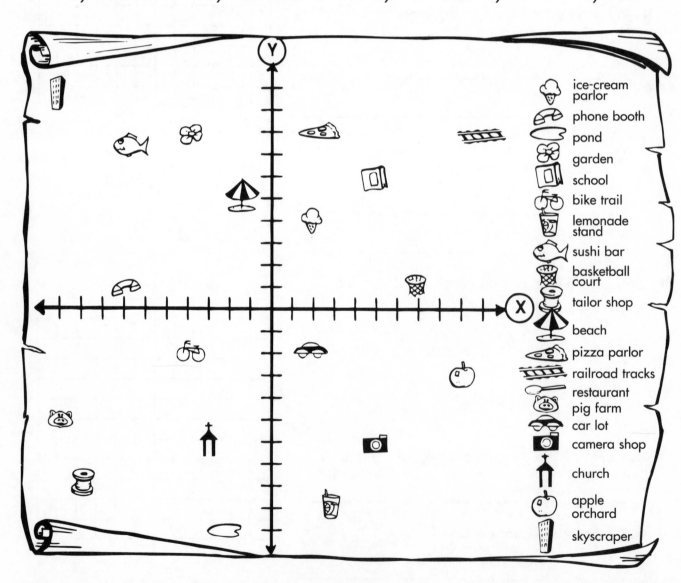

Equations in Context

1. Estelle wants to buy a set of dishes at an auction. She will owe a 5% buyer's commission as well as a 6.5% sales tax on the price of the dishes.

   a. Write an equation expressing the total cost, C, of her purchase if she bids p dollars on the dishes.

   b. If she has $300, what is the largest amount she can bid on the dishes?

2. One car rental agency charges a flat fee of $50 plus $0.25 per mile. Another charges a flat fee of $40 plus $0.40 per mile.

   a. For each agency, write an equation expressing the cost, C, of traveling m miles.
      Agency 1: $C =$
      Agency 2: $C =$

   b. If you plan on traveling 115 miles total, which is the better deal? What if you plan on traveling only 65 miles?

   c. Use agency ____ if you plan on traveling less than ____ miles. Use agency ____ if you plan on traveling more than ____ miles.

3. Akim wants to sell his coin collection. Golden Hammer Auction House charges a 15% commission. Heavy Gavel Auction House charges a listing fee of $500 and only a 12% commission.

   a. For each auction house, write an equation expressing the commission price, C, if the collection sells for p dollars.
      Golden Hammer: $C =$
      Heavy Gavel: $C =$

   b. If the coins sell for $25,000, which firm should Akim use?

Building Expressions

The Trivets-by-Tom Company makes frames for square trivets from 1-inch pieces of tile. Tom, the owner, asked four of his employees to submit diagrams that would show the number of tiles needed for any size of square trivet (side measured in inches).

▶ Use each diagram to write an expression for the number of tiles needed to frame a trivet with a side of T inches.

1. Tamika's Diagram

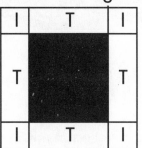

_____

2. Todd's Diagram

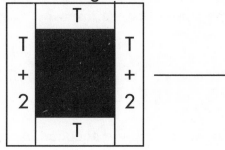

_____

3. Terence's Diagram

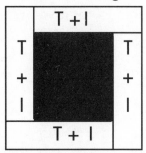

_____

4. Tanesha's Diagram

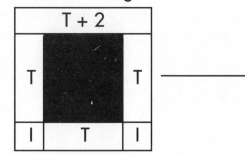

_____

5. What happens when you simplify each expression?

_____

_____

6. How many tiles would be needed for the frame of a square trivet with side measure T equal to:

a. 3 in.? _____

b. 4 in.? _____

c. 5 in.? _____

d. 6 in.? _____

e. 10 in.? _____

Critical Thinking

▶ Be a "critical problem solver" as you try to solve the following problems. The problems may not be as difficult as they initially appear. Look at the problem from a different point of view. There may be unnecessary information.

1. Booky, the bookworm, burrowed in a straight line from the last page of Vol. 1 to the first page of Vol. 2 of a collection kept in perfect order on a shelf. How far did he burrow if the bindings are each $\frac{1}{8}$ inch thick and the pages of each book are 2 inches thick?

2. Two truckers drove from Dayton to Toledo and back. The first trucker drove to Toledo at 50 mph and returned to Dayton at 60 mph. The second trucker drove to Toledo and back at 55 mph. If the round trip is 300 miles, which driver took longer to make the round trip?

3. You are trying to walk to school on a very icy sidewalk. The school is 100 yards from your house. For every step you take (1 ft.), you slide back 2 ft. You decide it is hopeless, so you turn around and go home. What happens?

4. A test track for new cars is one mile around. For the first lap, the driver averages 30 mph. How fast does the car have to travel a second lap to average 60 mph for the two laps?

5. Mary noticed that it takes 6 seconds for the town clock to strike 6:00. At lunch it takes more than 12 seconds to strike 12:00. If the clock has not slowed down, how long does it take for the clock to strike?

6. A water lily doubles itself each day. From the time it was placed in a pond until the surface of the pond (600 sq. ft.) was completely covered took 30 days. How long did it take for the pond to be half-covered?

Classifying Objects

1. These are gizmos.   These are not gizmos.   Which of these are gizmos?

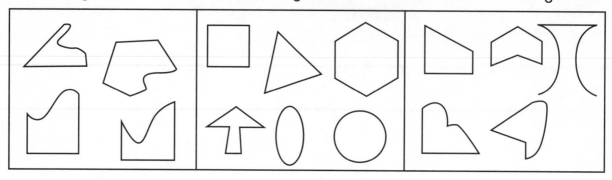

2. These are whatsits.   These are not whatsits.   Which of these are whatsits?

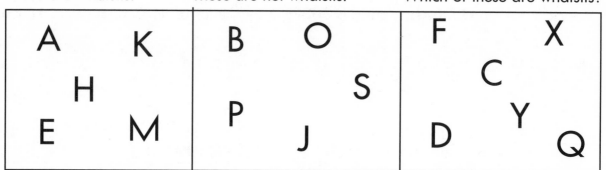

3. These are whatchamacallits.   These are not whatchamacallits.   Which of these are whatchamacallits?

2   11
    5
 3   7
	9 15
	      8
	 10 32
		17 23 51
		    34
		 6 19

4. Make up your own puzzle.

These are doodads.   These are not doodads.   Which of these are doodads?

    0-7424-1723-9 *Math*

Identifying Geometric Terms

▶ Write the letter of the shape next to its correct name.

A.

_____ **1.** Perpendicular Lines

B.

_____ **2.** Pyramid

C.

_____ **3.** Cylinder

D.

_____ **4.** Parallel Lines

E.

_____ **5.** Intersecting Lines

F.

_____ **6.** Sphere

G.

_____ **7.** Parallelogram

H.

_____ **8.** Cone

I.

_____ **9.** Right Triangle

J.

_____ **10.** Prism

 0-7424-1723-9 *Math*

Angle Sums and Triangles

The three angle measures of a triangle have a sum of 180 degrees. Two adjacent angles that form a straight line have an angle sum of 180 degrees.

▶ Without measuring, determine the measure of each indicated angle in the diagram below.

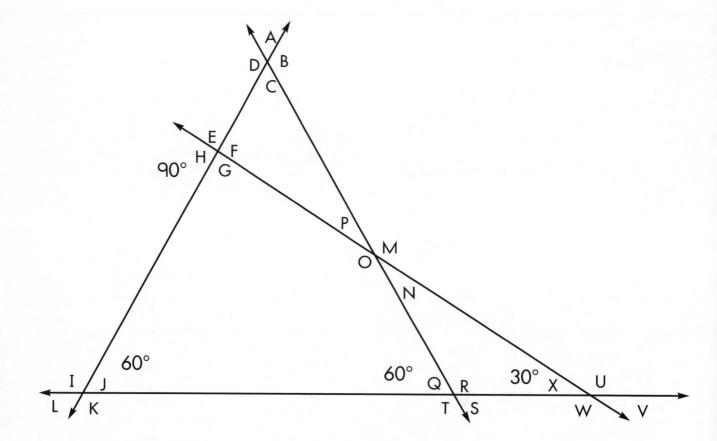

A. _____	**G.** _____	**M.** _____	**S.** _____
B. _____	**H.** 90°	**N.** _____	**T.** 120°
C. _____	**I.** _____	**O.** _____	**U.** _____
D. _____	**J.** 60°	**P.** _____	**V.** _____
E. _____	**K.** _____	**Q.** 60°	**W.** _____
F. _____	**L.** _____	**R.** _____	**X.** 30°

Quadrilaterals

▶ Place the terms in the diagram. Use each term only once.

square, quadrilateral, rhombus, rectangle, parallelogram, trapezoid

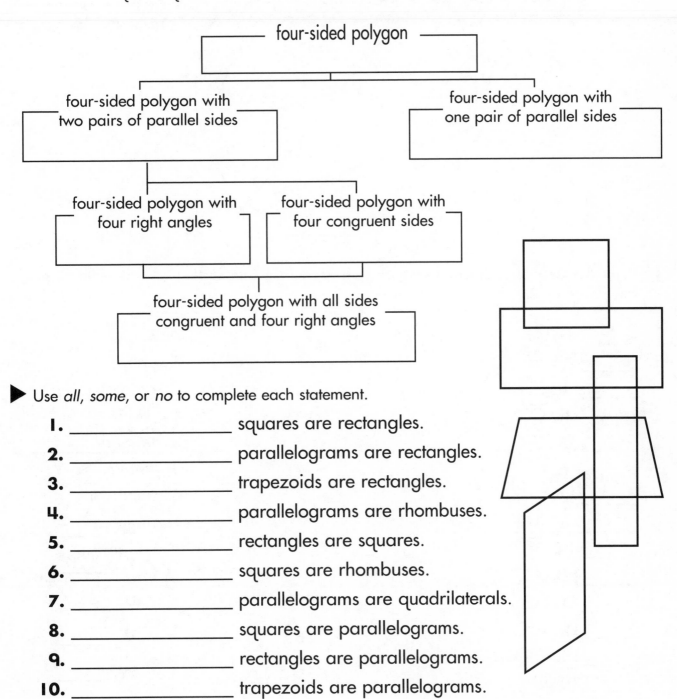

▶ Use *all*, *some*, or *no* to complete each statement.

1. _____ squares are rectangles.

2. _____ parallelograms are rectangles.

3. _____ trapezoids are rectangles.

4. _____ parallelograms are rhombuses.

5. _____ rectangles are squares.

6. _____ squares are rhombuses.

7. _____ parallelograms are quadrilaterals.

8. _____ squares are parallelograms.

9. _____ rectangles are parallelograms.

10. _____ trapezoids are parallelograms.

Parts of a Circle

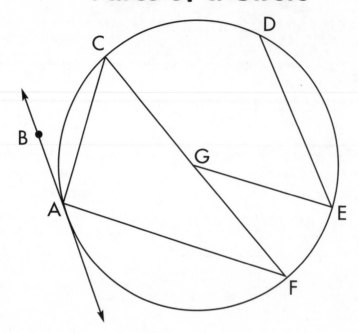

▶ Write the letter of each term next to the corresponding part of the circle. Some terms may be used more than once.

_____ 1. $\overset{\frown}{AF}$

_____ 2. $\overline{AF}$

_____ 3. $\overset{\frown}{CD}$

_____ 4. $\overline{CG}$

_____ 5. $\overset{\frown}{CDF}$

_____ 6. $\overline{CF}$

_____ 7. $\angle EGF$

_____ 8. $\overset{\frown}{ACF}$

_____ 9. $\overleftrightarrow{AB}$

_____ 10. $\overline{AC}$

_____ 11. $\overset{\frown}{AEC}$

_____ 12. $\angle CAF$

_____ 13. $\angle GED$

_____ 14. G

_____ 15. $\overset{\frown}{CAF}$

A. center

B. chord

C. diameter

D. radius

E. tangent

F. semicircle

G. minor arc

H. major arc

I. central angle

J. inscribed angle

Classifying Polyhedrons

Different types of pyramids and prisms are identified by the polygon used as the base.

Rectangular Prism

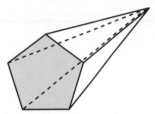

(Bases are rectangles.)

Pentagonal Pyramid

(Base is a pentagon.)

▶ Write the name of each prism below.

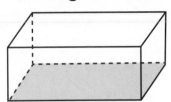

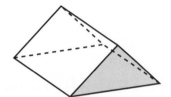

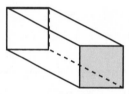

1. _____   2. _____   3. _____

▶ Write the name of each pyramid below.

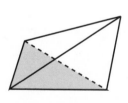

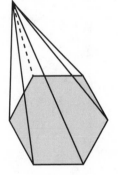

4. _____   5. _____   6. _____

▶ Write the name of each polyhedron below.

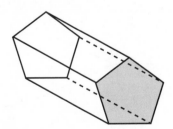

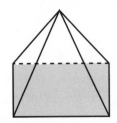

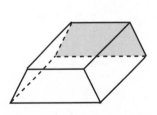

7. _____   8. _____   9. _____

0-7424-1723-9 *Math*

Similar Triangles

Corresponding angles of similar triangles are congruent. Corresponding sides are in proportion.

$\triangle ABC \sim \triangle DEF$

$m\angle A = m\angle D,\ m\angle B = m\angle E,\ m\angle C = m\angle F$

$\frac{a}{d} = \frac{b}{e} = \frac{c}{f}.$

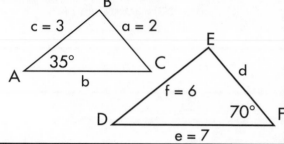

Find the measures of the remaining angles.

Since $m\angle A = 35°$, $m\angle D = 35°$.

We know $m\angle F = m\angle C = 70°$.

Therefore, $m\angle E = m\angle B = 180 - (35 + 70) = 75°$.

Find the lengths of the remaining sides.

First, use $\frac{a}{d} = \frac{c}{f}$. $\frac{2}{d} = \frac{3}{6}$

$12 = 3d \rightarrow 4 = d$

Then, use $\frac{b}{e} = \frac{c}{f}$: $\frac{b}{7} = \frac{3}{6}$

$6b = 21 \rightarrow b = 3.5$

▶ For each pair of triangles, $\triangle ABC \sim \triangle DEF$. Write the missing side lengths and angle measurements on the diagrams.

1.

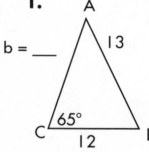
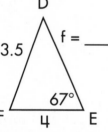

2.

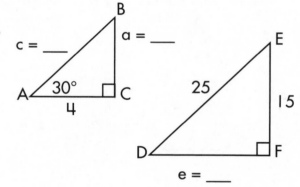

3.   **4.**

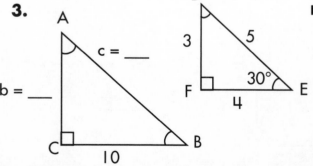
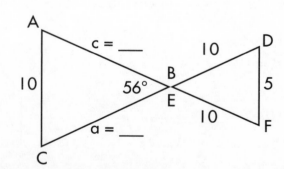

0-7424-1723-9 *Math*

Name_____ Date _____ Geometry

Similar Figures and Perimeter

In similar figures, the ratio of the perimeter is equal to the ratio of any pair of sides.

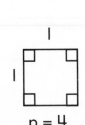

$\frac{1}{2}$ = sides ratio

$\frac{4}{8}$ = $\frac{1}{2}$ = perimeter ratio

▶ Find the missing perimeter, ratio, or labeled side (all figures are similar).

1.

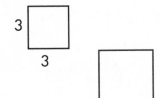

ratio = $\frac{2}{3}$

P = _____

2.

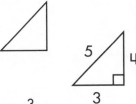

ratio = $\frac{3}{4}$

P = _____

3.

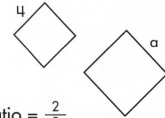

ratio = $\frac{2}{3}$

a = _____

4.

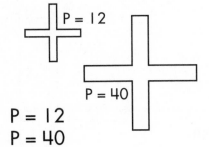

P = 12
P = 40

ratio = _____

5.

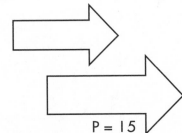

ratio = $\frac{3}{5}$

P = _____

6.

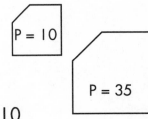

P = 10
P = 35

ratio = _____

0-7424-1723-9 *Math*

Pythagorean Theorem

The **Pythagorean Theorem** illustrates the following relationship among the three sides of a right triangle:

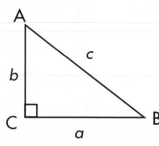

$$a^2 + b^2 = c^2 \qquad\qquad leg^2 + leg^2 = hypotenuse^2$$

▶ Use the Pythagorean Theorem to find the missing side.

1.

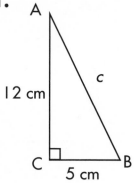

12 cm c 5 cm

2.

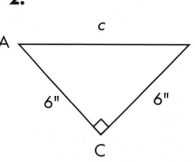

c 6" 6"

3.

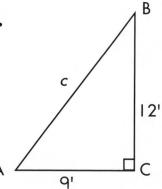

c 12' 9'

4.

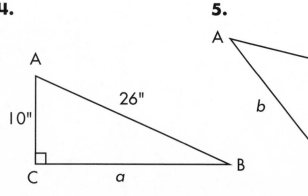

26" 10" a

5.

25 cm b 15 cm

6.

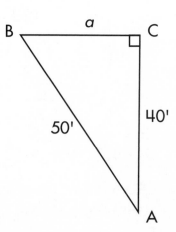

a 50' 40'

Angle Sums of Polygons

The fact that the three angles of a triangle total
180° can be used to determine the angle sum of any polygon.

What is the angle sum of polygon ABCDE?

3 x 180° = 540°

▶ Draw diagonals to divide each polygon into triangles. Calculate the angle sum of each polygon.

1.  _____

2.  _____

3.  _____

4. 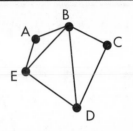 _____

5. 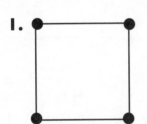 _____

6. 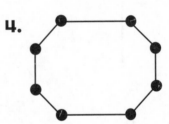 _____

7.  _____

8.  _____

9. Write an equation showing the relationship between the number of sides (N) and the number of triangles (T) in a polygon. _____

10. Write a formula for the angle sum (S) in terms of (N). _____

Transformations

Translation (Slide)	**Rotation** (Turn)	**Reflection** (Flip)

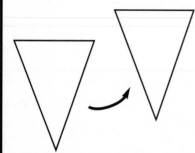 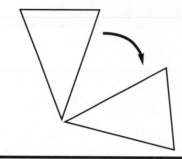 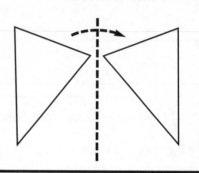

▶ Which single basic motion will make these figures coincide?

1.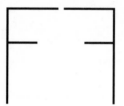

2.

3.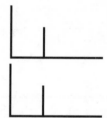

4.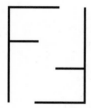

5.

6.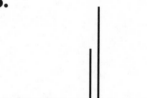

7.

8.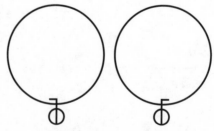

9.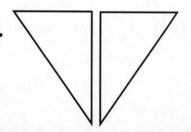

10.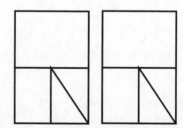

0-7424-1723-9 *Math*

Rotation Around an Axis

When a figure is rotated around an axis, it creates a solid, where only a two-dimensional figure had previously existed. Look at the figure below.

If the circle in the figure above were spun around the axis line as indicated, a figure resembling a solid ring would be created.

▶ For each of the figures below, draw a sketch of that figure as it would look after being rotated around the axis as indicated.

1.

2.

3.

4.

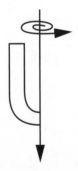

0-7424-1723-9 *Math*

Coordinate Grid Transformations

▶ **1.** Draw a triangle with vertices A(-2, 2), B(3, -4), and C(-1, -2).

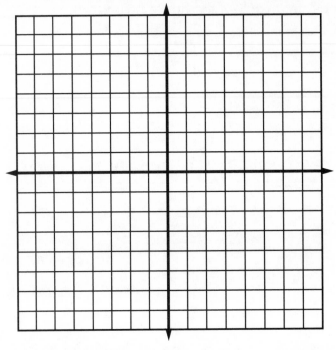

2. Add 3 to each x-coordinate of △ABC and draw △DEF.
   D (___,___), E (___,___), F (___,___).

3. Compare △ABC and △DEF. _____

4. Add -4 to each x-coordinate of △ABC and draw △GHI.
   G (___,___), H (___,___), I (___,___).

5. Compare △ABC and △GHI. _____

6. Add 3 to each y-coordinate of △ABC and draw △JKL.
   J (___,___), K (___,___), L (___,___).

7. Compare △ABC and △JKL. _____

8. Add -4 to each y-coordinate of △ABC and draw △MNO.
   M (___,___), N (___,___), O (___,___).

9. Compare △ABC and △MNO. _____

Coordinate Grid Transformations

A **transformation** is a rule for moving a figure to a new location. **Slides** (translations), **turns** (rotations), and **flips** (reflections) maintain the figure size.

▶ Use the grids to show the indicated transformations. Label corresponding points.

1. Slide 3 units right and 2 units down.

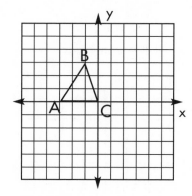

2. Turn 90° clockwise about P.

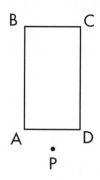

3. Flip over the y-axis.

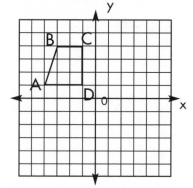

4. Slide 6 units left and 4 units up.

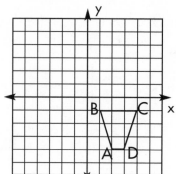

5. Turn 180° counterclockwise about P.

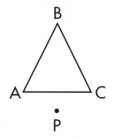

6. Flip over the x-axis.

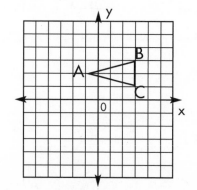

Point of View

▶ Two-dimensional drawings can be used to show top, front, and side views of three-dimensional objects.

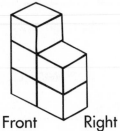

Front   Right

Top   Front   Right Side

▶ Use the grid to draw the top, front, and right side views of the given figure.

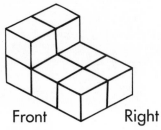

Front   Right

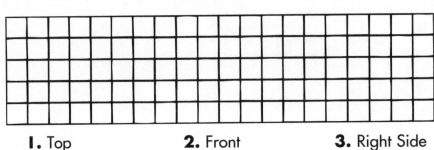

I. Top   **2.** Front   **3.** Right Side

▶ Use the dot grids to draw the figures based on the top, front, and side views.

4.

Top   Front   Right Side

4.

5.

Top   Front   Right Side

5.

Nets

A **net** is a pattern that can be folded to cover a solid figure. The area of the unfolded net equals the surface area of the solid figure.

▶ Match the net with its solid.

1. _____ 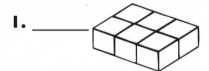   **2.** _____    **3.** _____

A. 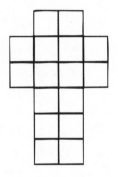   **B.** 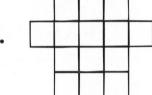   **C.**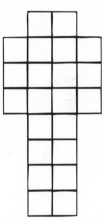

▶ If each square represents 1 cm², find the surface area of each solid.

4. Area #1 = _____ cm²   **5.** Area #2 = _____ cm²   **6.** Area #3 = _____ cm²

7. Which pattern is a net for a cube?

A.    **B.** 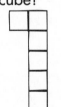   **C.** 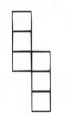   **D.**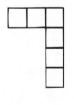

8. Draw a net on the grid for the rectangular prism shown. Then calculate its surface area.

    Net: 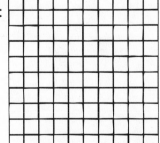   Area:

Perimeter and Area: Triangles and Trapezoids

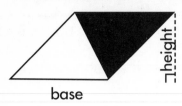

1. The area of the triangle is _____ the area of the parallelogram.

2. The area of a triangle = _____ x base x height.

base

▶ Find the area of each triangle. Include the appropriate units.

3.
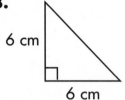
6 cm
6 cm

4.
14 mm 30 mm
16 mm

5.
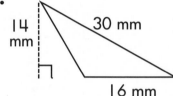
4 in.
12 in.

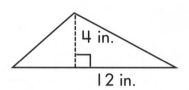

X b Y
h
W B Z

6. The area of the trapezoid XYZW equals the area of △XYZ _____ the area of △ZWX.

7. The area of the trapezoid equals $\frac{1}{2}$ x b x h _____ $\frac{1}{2}$ x B x h.

8. Using the distributive property, the equation becomes: area of a trapezoid = $\frac{1}{2}$ h(b _____ B).

▶ Find the areas of the trapezoids. Include the appropriate units.

9.
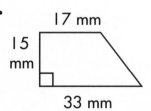
17 mm
15 mm
33 mm

10.
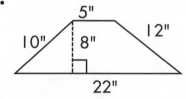
5"
10" 8" 12"
22"

11.
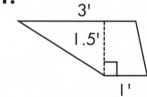
3'
1.5'
1'

Circumference and Area of Circles

d = diameter, r = radius, $\pi \approx 3.14$

Circumference:
$C = \pi d$

Area:
$A = \pi r^2$

▶ Find the circumference and area of each circle. Include the correct units. Round to the nearest hundredth.

1.

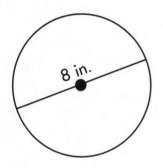

8 in.

2.

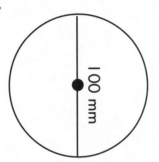

100 mm

3.

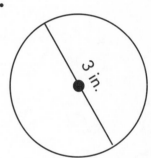

3 in.

4.

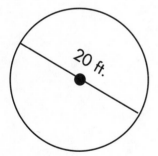

20 ft.

5.

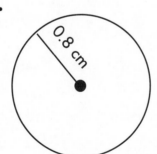

0.8 cm

6.

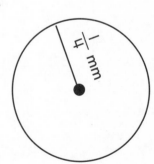

$\frac{1}{4}$ mm

7.

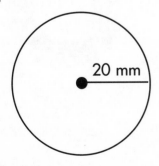

20 mm

8.

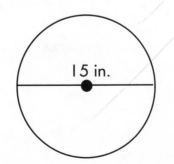

15 in.

9.

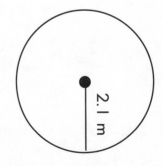

2.1 m

0-7424-1723-9 *Math*

Area of Irregular Shapes

$$\text{Area}_{\text{rectangle}} = l \times w; \quad \text{Area}_{\text{triangle}} = \frac{1}{2} bh; \quad \text{Area}_{\text{circle}} = \pi r^2$$

▶ Divide the figures below into rectangles, triangles, and circles to find the areas.

1.

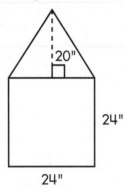

20"
24"
24"

2.

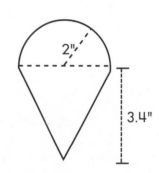

12'
14'
18'
16'

3.

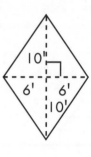

10"
6' 6'
10'

4.

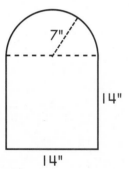

7"
14"
14"

5.

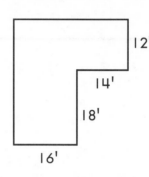

2"
3.4"

6.

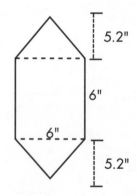

5.2"
6"
6"
5.2"

▶ Add or subtract areas to find the area of the shaded regions.

7.

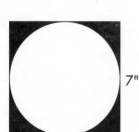

7"

8.

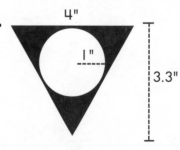

4"
1"
3.3"

9.

1'
4'

10. How much greater is the area of a 4-inch square than a 4-inch diameter circle?

_____

0-7424-1723-9 *Math*

Volume of Prisms and Cylinders

Volume = Base Area x Height

Triangular Prism	**Cylinder**
Base Area = $\frac{1}{2}$ bh = $\frac{1}{2}$ x 6 x 4 = 12 in.^{2}	Base Area = πr^2 = π x (15 in.)^2 = 706.5 in.^{2}
Volume = Base Area x Height of Prism	Volume = Base Area x Height of Cylinder
= 12 in.^{2} x 12 in. = 144 in.^{3}	= 706.5 in.^{2} x 20 in. = 14,130 in.^{3}

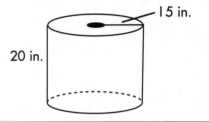

▶ Find the volume of each figure. Round to the nearest hundredth. Use π = 3.14.

1.

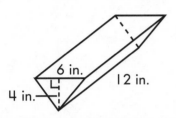

5 cm
15 cm
14 cm

2.

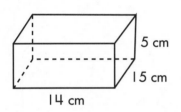

16 m
0.5 m
8 m

3.

3.2 ft.
2.1 ft.
1.9 ft.

4.

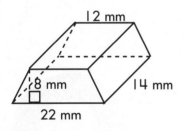

12 mm
8 mm
14 mm
22 mm

5.

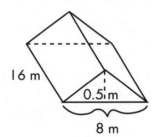

21 cm
6 cm

6.

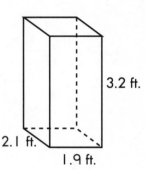

3 m
5 m

7.

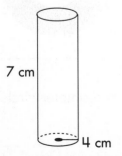

7 cm
4 cm

8.

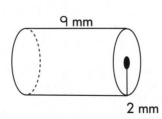

9 mm
2 mm

9.

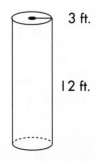

3 ft.
12 ft.

0-7424-1723-9 *Math*

Volume of Pyramids and Cones

Volume = $\frac{1}{3}$ x Base Area x Height

Square Pyramid	Cone
Base Area = $b^2 = 6^2 = 36$ cm^2	Base Area = $\pi r^2 = \pi \times (5\text{ cm})^2 = 78.5$ cm^2
Volume = $\frac{1}{3}$ Base Area x Height of Pyramid	Volume = $\frac{1}{3}$ Base Area x Height of Cone
$= \frac{1}{3} \times 36$ cm^2 x 4 cm = 48 cm^3	$= \frac{1}{3} \times 78.5$ cm^2 x 12 cm = 314 cm^3

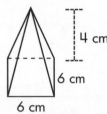

4 cm
6 cm
6 cm

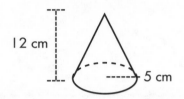

12 cm
5 cm

▶ Find the volume of the following figures. Round to the nearest hundredth. Use π = 3.14.

1.

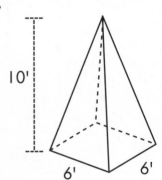

10'
6'   6'

_____

2.

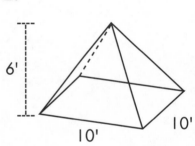

6'
10'   10'

_____

3.

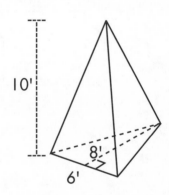

10'
8'
6'

_____

4.

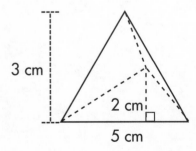

3 cm
2 cm
5 cm

_____

5.

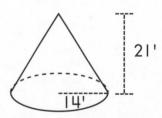

21'
14'

_____

6.

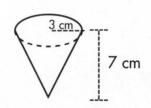

3 cm
7 cm

_____

Surface Area

The **surface area** of a three-dimensional object is found by adding the areas of each of its faces.

▶ Find the surface area of each figure.

1.

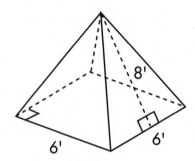

8'
6'   6'

2.

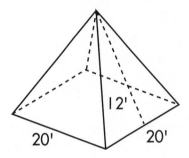

12'
20'   20'

3.

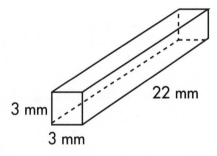

22 mm
3 mm
3 mm

4.

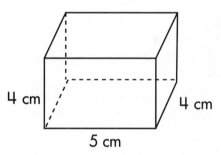

4 cm   4 cm
5 cm

5.

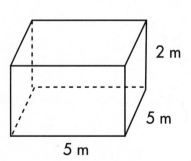

2 m
5 m
5 m

6.

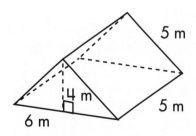

5 m
4 m
6 m
5 m

Scale Factors: Area

1. The following rectangles are similar, with a scale factor of 1:3.

2 cm [ ]
6 cm

w =
l =

a. w = _____ l = _____
b. area of small rectangle = _____
c. area of large rectangle = _____
d. When the scale factor is 1:3, the area of the large rectangle is _____ times greater than the area of the small rectangle.

2. The following triangles are similar with a scale factor of 1:4.

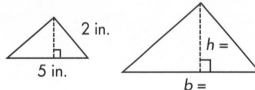

2 in.
5 in.
h =
b =

a. b = _____ h = _____
b. Area of small triangle = _____
c. Area of large triangle = _____
d. When the scale factor is 1:4, the area of the large triangle is _____ times greater than the area of the small triangle.

3. On a separate piece of paper, sketch and label the base and height of two similar parallelograms with a scale factor of 1:5. Find their areas and then complete the statement below.
When the scale factor is 1:5, the area of the large parallelogram is _____ times greater than the area of the small parallelogram.

▶ Look for patterns in your results from problems 1-3 to help answer the following questions.

4. When the scale factor of two similar figures is 1:k, the area of the large figure is _____ times greater than the area of the small figure.

5. Two hexagons are similar with a scale factor of 1:15. The area of the small hexagon is 8 cm². The area of the larger hexagon is _____ .

6. Two trapezoids are similar with a scale factor of 1:8. The area of the small trapezoid is 10 cm². The area of the larger trapezoid is _____ .

Scale Factors: Volume

1. The following square prisms are similar, with a scale factor of 1:3.

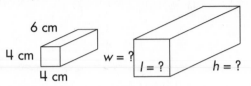

6 cm

4 cm

4 cm

w = ?

l = ?

h = ?

a. w = _____ l = _____ h = _____

b. volume of small prism = _____

c. volume of large prism = _____

d. When the scale factor is 1:3, the volume of the large prism is _____ times greater than the volume of the small prism.

2. The following triangular pyramids are similar with a scale factor of 1:4.

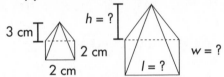

h = ?

3 cm

2 cm

2 cm

w = ?

l = ?

a. w = _____ l = _____ h = _____

b. volume of small pyramid = _____

c. volume of large pyramid = _____

d. When the scale factor is 1:4, the volume of the large pyramid is _____ times greater than the area of the small pyramid.

3. On a separate piece of paper, sketch and label the radius and height of two similar cylinders with a scale factor of 1:5. Find their volumes and then complete the statement below. When the scale factor is 1:5, the volume of the large cylinder is _____ times greater than the volume of the small cylinder.

▶ Look for patterns in your results from problems 1-3 to help answer the following questions.

4. When the scale factor of two similar figures is 1:K, the volume of the large figure is _____ times greater than the volume of the small figure.

5. Two hexagonal prisms are similar with a scale factor of 1:15. The volume of the small hexagonal prism is 8 cm³. The volume of the larger hexagonal prism is _____ .

6. Two spheres are similar with a scale factor of 1:8. The volume of the small sphere is 10 cm³. The volume of the larger sphere is _____ .

Scale Factors in Context

▶ A scale model of a building shaped like a rectangular
prism stands 2 ft. long, 1 ft. wide, and 4 ft. tall.

4 ft.

1 ft.   2 ft.

1. The building is to be built on a scale of $\frac{20}{1}$ with its model.

    a. What are the dimensions of the building? _____

    b. The outer walls of the building will be made of brick.
    How many square feet of brick should be bought? _____

    c. What is the volume of the building? _____

2. It turns out more space was needed than originally thought. The scale factor is changed to $\frac{25}{1}$.

    a. What are the dimensions of the actual building? _____

    b. The outer walls of the building will be made of brick. How many square feet of brick
    should be bought? _____

    c. What is the volume of the building? _____

3. Architects are examining the results of using different scale factors to build the actual
building. Answer each question below and then write equations to show the
relationships between the scale factor, *k*, and the measurements of the actual building.

    a. How will the dimensions of the building compare to those of the scale model?

        $h =$ _____ $w =$ _____ $l =$ _____

    b. How will the area of the building's walls compare to that of the scale model? _____

        $A =$ _____

    c. How will the volume of the building compare to that of the scale model?

        $V =$ _____

Measurement in Context

1. Bonnie is planning to carry a rectangular poster at a demonstration. She has the choice of poster board in two sizes. The larger poster board has dimensions of 56 cm by 76 cm. The smaller poster board has dimensions of 35 cm by 50 cm.

   a. How many more square centimeters of area per side does the larger poster offer?

   b. The larger poster board is priced at $3.89 while the smaller poster board is priced at $2.89. Which board represents a better cost per square centimeter?

2. A box with dimensions of 18 inches by 18 inches by 24 inches is full of loose plastic packing material shaped like peanuts.

   a. Would a cylindrical container that is 26 inches tall with a radius of 8 inches be large enough to hold all of the packing material? Explain.

   b. What is the difference in volume between the two containers?

3. Jamal is buying a group of solar power panels. He knows that a minimum of 24 square feet of panels are needed for generating the power he needs. The panels come in two sizes: 18 inches by 30 inches or 24 inches by 36 inches.

   a. If he buys the smaller-size panels, how many will he need?

   b. If he buys the larger-size panels, how many will he need?

   c. The smaller panels cost $42.89 each and the larger panels cost $71.20 each. Which size offers the better deal per square foot?

4. Griffin took a storage box with a height of 20 inches and cut off a 4-inch strip all the way around, reducing the height of the box. If the box could hold 2,000 cubic inches of material before the strip was removed, how much can it hold now?

Converting Standard Measurements

Standard Measures Conversion Chart

Weight
1 pound (lb.) = 16 ounces (oz.)
1 ton (T.) = 2,000 pounds

Length
1 foot = 12 inches (in.)
1 yard (yd.) = 3 feet (ft.)
1 mile (mi.) = 5,280 feet

Capacity
1 tablespoon (tbsp.) = 3 teaspoons (tsp.)
1 cup (c.) =   16 tablespoons = 8 fluid ounces (fl. oz.)
1 pint (pt.) =   2 cups
1 quart (qt.) =   2 pints
1 gallon (gal.) =   4 quarts

► Convert the following measurements.

1. 2 gal. = _____ qt.

2. 5 T. = _____ lb.

3. 128 oz. = _____ lb.

4. 12 c. = _____ pt.

5. 16 qt. = _____ gal.

6. 2.3 yd. = _____ in.

7. 96,000 oz. = _____ T.

8. 3 lb. = _____ oz.

9. 5 pt. = _____ tbsp.

10. 15,840 ft. = _____ mi.

11. 51 yd. = _____ in.

12. 7 ft. = _____ in.

13. 3,072 tsp. = _____ gal.

14. 7 gal. = _____ tbsp.

15. 7 mi. = _____ in.

Metric Measures

> The **meter** is the basic unit of length.
> The **liter** is the basic unit of liquid capacity.
> The **gram** is the basic unit of mass.

The basic unit of meters is often expressed in terms of kilometers (1,000 meters) and, for smaller measures, centimeters ($\frac{1}{100}$ of a meter).

The basic unit of liters is often expressed in terms of milliliters ($\frac{1}{1000}$ of a liter).

The basic unit of grams is often expressed in terms of kilograms (1,000 grams) and, for smaller measures, milligrams ($\frac{1}{1000}$ of a gram).

▶ For each situation below, state the most appropriate unit of measure.

1. the length of a pencil _____

2. the weight of a medium-sized dog _____

3. the amount of water a cooler will hold _____

4. a small dose of cough syrup _____

5. the distance between 2 cities _____

6. the weight of a letter being sent _____

7. the amount of fuel a car's gas tank will hold _____

8. the weight of a hummingbird _____

9. the height of a small child _____

10. the weight of a block of cheese _____

0-7424-1723-9 *Math*

Converting Metric Measurements

Metric Conversions

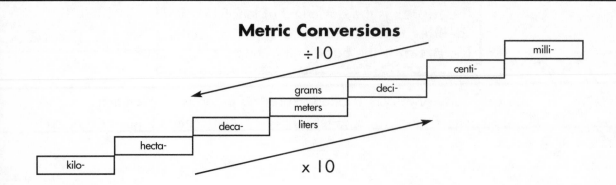

÷ 10

× 10

Multiply when moving up on the chart—from kilometers to meters or from meters to centimeters. Divide when moving down on the chart—from millimeters to decimeters or from meters to hectameters.

Smaller Units to Larger Units	**Larger Units to Smaller Units**
2,300 mm = _____ m	_____ cL = 2 hL
To get from millimeters to meters you must move down three stairs. So, divide by 10^3 (or 1,000).	To get from hectaliters to centiliters you must move up 4 stairs. So, multiply by 10^4 (or 10,000).
2,300 mm ÷ 1,000 = 2.3 m	2 hL × 10,000 = 20,000 cL

▶ Use the chart to help you convert the metric units.

1. 40 m = _____cm   **2.** 16 m = _____mm   **3.** 2,400 cm = _____m

4. 5,340 m = _____km   **5.** 824 hm = _____dam **6.** 16.8 hL = _____cL

7. 0.06 hL = _____mL   **8.** 0.08 L = _____cL   **9.** 0.06 daL = _____cL

10. 25 L = _____dL   **11.** 7.2 kg = _____dg   **12.** 11.01 g = _____mg

13. 16.013 kg = _____dag **14.** 0.062 g = _____cg **15.** 310 hg = _____g

Converting Between Systems

1 mile = 1.6 kilometers	
1 kilogram = 2.2 pounds	

Smaller Units to Larger Units	**Larger Units to Smaller Units**
74.8 lb. = _____kg	14 mi. = _____km
1 kg = 2.2 lb.	1 mi. = 1.6 km
74.8 ÷ 2.2 = 34	×14 ×14
74.8 lb. = 34 kg	14 mi. = 22.4 km

▶ Convert the following measurements.

1. 3 mi. = ____km

2. 12 lb. = ____kg

3. 8 km = ____mi.

4. 6.6 lb. = ____kg

5. 210 lb. = ____kg

6. 10 mi. = ____km

7. 3.2 km = ____mi.

8. 9.6 km = ____mi.

9. 79.2 lb. = ____kg

▶ Compare the following measurements using <, >, or =.

10. 50 lb.   23 kg

11. 9 mi.   13 km

12. 7 mi.   11.2 km

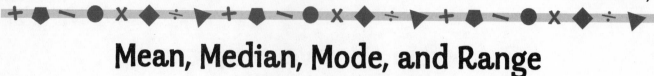

Mean, Median, Mode, and Range

The **mean** (or average) is found by dividing the sum by the number of data values. When the data is arranged in numerical order, the middle one is the **median**. The value that occurs most frequently is the **mode**. The **range** is the difference between the greatest and the least value.

Mike's test scores in spelling were 94, 88, 72, 90, 70, 89, and 70.

1. What was his mean score? _____

2. What was his median score? _____

3. What was his mode score? _____

4. Which score (mean, median, mode) do you think he would like to see on his report card? Why? _____

5. What was the range of Mike's spelling scores? _____

The chef at Bistro Café found it challenging to satisfy all his diners. The ages of the diners one evening were as follows: 87, 58, 54, 61, 3, 35, 31, 28, 3, 16, and 68.

6. What is the mean age? _____

7. What is the median age? _____

8. What is the mode? _____

9. Based on the mean age, what should the chef serve, steak and lobster or macaroni and cheese? _____

10. Based on the mode age, what should be served? _____

Mean, Median, Mode, and Range

Twelve students at Park High School were asked how many books they read in the past year. They responded with the following totals:

45, 38, 25, 59, 101, 49, 87, 75, 77, 59, 48, 81

▶ Use the students' totals to answer the questions.

1. What is the mean of these numbers?

_____

2. Write these numbers in order from least to greatest in the chart to the right.

3. What is the mode? _____

4. What is the median? _____

5. What is the range of these numbers?

_____

6. Why do you think the range of these numbers is so great?

_____

_____

7. How many books do YOU read in a year?

_____

Order	Number
1	
2	
3	
4	
5	
6	
7	
8	
9	
10	
11	
12	

Statistical Experiments

> Statistical experiments involve collecting,
> organizing, and analyzing data.

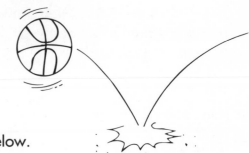

Ms. Forester's class is interested in holding a winter
intramural sports tournament for the whole school.
To collect data on game preferences, they surveyed
all 435 students in the school. They noted the results below.

Favorite Games

Intramural Choices	Number of Votes
Ping-Pong	57
Basketball	63
Kickball	32
Tennis	78
Badminton	7
Golf	53
Volleyball	84

1. List the games in order from the most popular to the least.

_____

2. Based on this data, which five games should they play?

_____

3. Which game should definitely not be part of the tournament?

_____

4. Do the number of votes justify holding an intramural tournament?
Why or why not? _____

5. What is the mean? _____

6. What is the mode? _____

7. What is the median? _____

8. What is the range? _____

Statistical Experiments

The student council members would like to sponsor a "Fun Night" at school, but are not sure what night to schedule it or whether or not the students want one. They decided to run a survey in the school newspaper to collect data.

The results are:

Good idea	195
Bad idea	30
Monday evening	10
Tuesday evening	17
Wednesday evening	0
Thursday evening	53
Friday evening	145

Total School Population: 237

Answer the following questions based on the collected data.

1. Is having a "Fun Night" a good idea? Why or why not?

_____

2. Which night would be best? _____

3. Which night would be the second choice? _____

4. Do the number of votes justify the results of the survey? Explain.

_____

5. Which night should not be chosen at all? _____

6. If parents were surveyed, do you think they would choose the same night? Why or why not?

_____

Variation

Raúl and Olívia are paid based on commission.

Commissions

Employee	M	T	W	T	F
Raúl	$205	$200	$210	$185	$200
Olívia	$0	$310	$200	$200	$290

The mean, the median, and the mode of each employee's commissions all equal $200. These measures do not indicate that Raúl's commissions are more consistent than Olívia's commissions. Instead, we need to calculate measures of variation.

Range: the difference between the largest value and the smallest value.

1. Raúl _____

2. Olívia _____

Deviation: the distance of the values from the mean. For this situation, Mean = $200

3. Raúl _+5_, _____, _____, _−15_, _____

4. Olívia _____, _____, _____, _____, _____

Variance: the sum of the squared deviations of n items divided by $(n − 1)$.

5. a. Square the results from #3. Raúl: _25_, _____, _____, _____, _____

   b. Add the results from #5a and divide by $(5 − 1)$. _____

6. a. Square the results from #4 Olívia: _40,000_, _____, _____, _____, _____

   b. Add the results from #6a and divide by $(5 − 1)$. _____

Standard deviation: the positive square root of the variance. Use a calculator.

7. Find the square root (nearest 0.1) of the result from #5b. _____

8. Find the square root (nearest 0.1) of the result from #6b. _____

Circle the correct word. The greater the standard deviation, the _more/less_ consistent are the data values.

Interpolation

Estimating values between data values is called **interpolation.**

Hot water was poured into black and white cans. The temperature of each can was recorded every 5 minutes.

Minutes	Temperature °C	
	Black Can	White Can
0	98	98
5	72	90
10	48	74
15	39	62
20	30	53
25	27	44
30	24	38
35	22	33
40	21	29
45	20	25
50	20	22
55	20	20
60	20	20

From the data you can assume that between 0 and 5 minutes the temperature of the black can is between 98 and 72 degrees. At 2 minutes, the temperature would be approximately halfway between 72 and 98 (closer to the 98) or ≈ 87 degrees.

▶ Use the data table to determine approximate temperatures.

1. Temperature of the black can at

    a. 14 min. _____

    b. 27 min. _____

    c. 38 min. _____

    d. 41 min. _____

    e. 51 min. _____

2. Temperature of the white can at

    a. 14 min. _____

    b. 27 min. _____

    c. 38 min. _____

    d. 41 min. _____

    e. 51 min. _____

▶ Use the data table to determine approximate time.

3. Black can: **a.** 46 degrees _____   **b.** 37 degrees _____

4. White can: **a.** 46 degrees _____   **b.** 37 degrees _____

Double Line and Bar Graphs

Double line and **bar graphs** show a comparison between two similar types of data.

Body Mass (kg)	Calories Burned During 30 Minutes of Activity	
	Playing Basketball	Cycling
30	120	59
40	161	81
50	202	99
60	241	118

1. Create a double line graph to display the information in the table above. Label the vertical axis with an appropriate scale.

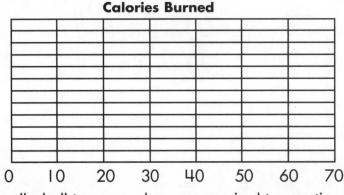

Calories Burned

Body Mass (Kg)

0   10   20   30   40   50   60   70

Playing Basketball

Cycling
– – – – – – – – – –

2. Each volleyball team member was required to practice serving 100 times each week. The table gives the frequency of successful serves for weeks 1 and 6. Construct a double bar graph showing the number of each girl's successful serves.

Frequency		
Name	Week 1	Week 6
Uyen	38	95
María	72	95
Jody	40	60
Suki	52	73
Latoya	34	72
Natasha	78	86

Week 1: ■

Week 2: □

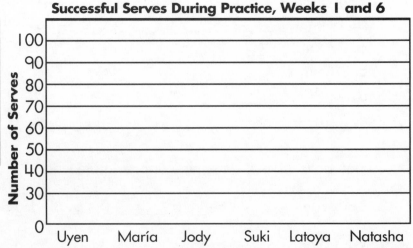

Successful Serves During Practice, Weeks 1 and 6

Number of Serves

100
90
80
70
60
50
40
30
0

Uyen   María   Jody   Suki   Latoya   Natasha

Name _____ Date _____

Frequency Tables and Histograms

Fran and Fred Franklin decided to sell some items at a flea market. The Franklins sold 40 items, ranging in price from $1 to $40. As items were bought, they wrote the amounts in a list.

1, 1, 39, 40, 2, 2, 5, 19, 20, 20, 5, 6, 8, 8, 8, 10, 10, 25, 29, 30, 10, 10, 11, 12,

12, 15, 5, 6, 15, 15, 18, 21, 22, 25, 25, 30, 36, 40, 2, 33

Fran and Fred wondered at which price range most items are bought. Fran started to organize the information into a frequency table.

1. Complete her table.

Fran's Frequency Table

Distribution of Flea Market Items		
Price Intervals	Tally	Frequency
$1 – $5		
$6 – $10		
$11 – $15		
$16 – $20	IIII	4
$21 – $25		
$26 – $30		
$31 – $35		
$36 – $40		

Fred wanted to see a graph of the information. He started to draw a frequency histogram.

2. Complete his histogram.

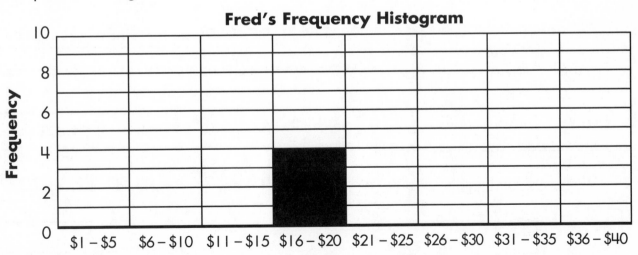

Fred's Frequency Histogram

3. In which price ranges were the greatest and least number of items sold? _____

Quartiles

Quartiles group data points into quarters—four equal parts.

Nineteen students had the following test results:
67, 75, 45, 89, 91, 70, 80, 85, 77, 62, 72, 95, 81, 76, 55, 59, 68, 88, 100

1. Arrange the test scores from least to greatest.

___ ___ ___ ___ ___ ___ ___ ___ ___ ___ ___ ___ ___ ___ ___ ___ ___ ___ ___

2. Find and circle the median (middle) of the scores. It is called the **second quartile.**
_____

3. Find and put an x on the median of the lower half of the scores. It is called the **first quartile**. _____

4. Find and draw a square around the median of the upper half of the scores. It is called the **third quartile**. _____

5. If your score is 85, is it in the **upper quartile** (greater than the third quartile)? _____

Percentiles group data points into hundredths.

▶ Follow these steps to find the percentile ranking for a test score of 85.

6. Find the total number of scores. _____

7. How many scores are less than or equal to your score? _____

8. Calculate the percent of scores (to the nearest 1%) that are less than or equal to your score. _____

9. Your score is in the _____ percentile. Your score is at least as good as the scores of _____ % of the scores.

10. a. Find the quartiles for the set of data. 67, 93, 88, 75, 99, 94, 81, 82, 76, 85, 79

Ist _____ 2nd _____ 3rd _____

b. Find the percentile for the score of 94. _____

Box Plots

A **box-and-whisker plot** can be used to show the spread of a set of data. The plot displays the median, the quartiles, and the range of the data values.

Data: 2, 2, 3, 3, 4, 6, 6, 7, 10, 10, 11, 12, 12, 18

Follow these steps to draw the box-and-whisker plot.
1. Write the values in numerical order.
2. Find the median and 1st and 3rd quartiles.
3. Make a number line with an even scale.
4. Draw a box between the first and third quartiles.
5. Draw a vertical line at the median.
6. Draw whiskers from the box to the extremes.

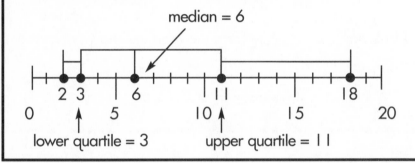

▶ Repeat steps 1-6 to make a box-and-whisker plot for each set of data.

A. 20, 34, 21, 24, 22, 25, 30, 30, 25, 40, 49, 26, 35, 36, 20

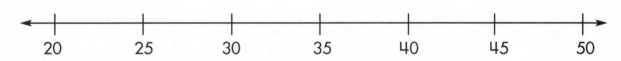

B. 22, 27, 30, 32, 40, 28, 49, 20, 28, 26, 23, 26, 26, 25, 24

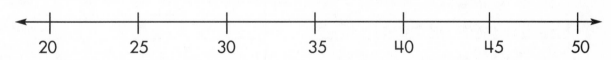

C. Compare and contrast the two box-and-whisker plots.

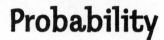

Probability

The **theoretical probability** that an event will occur is expressed as:

number of ways the event can occur.
total number of outcomes

Consider a bag containing this collection of red and white marbles.

(W) (W) (W) (R) (W) (R) (W) (W)

The theoretical probability of drawing a red is 2 out of 8 and the theoretical probability of drawing a white is 6 out of 8. Mathematicians use shorthand notation to mean "the probability of." The shorthand looks like this: P(E), where "E" represents the event being investigated.

The notation for the probabilities of drawing red or white from the marbles shown above are listed here.

$P(red) = \frac{2}{8}$ or 0.25 or 25% $P(white) = \frac{6}{8}$ or 0.75 or 75%

▶ Find the probability of drawing each color marble from the collection shown here. Give each answer as a fraction (in lowest terms), as a decimal (rounded to hundredths), and as a percent (round to the nearest percent).
NOTE: G is green, Y is yellow, and R is red.

(R) (G) (G) (G) (Y) (R) (G) (G) (G) (R) (G) (R)

	Fraction	Decimal	Percent
1. P (green) =			
2. P (pink) =			
3. P (yellow) =			
4. P (red or green) =			
5. P (red) =			
6. P (not green) =			

Probability

▶ What is the probability of rolling the following sums with two number cubes? Hint: There are 36 different number cube combinations.

1. seven _____

2. four _____

3. three _____

4. nine _____

5. doubles _____

6. eight _____

▶ With a standard deck of 52 cards, what is the probability of choosing each of the following cards? Express each answer as a fraction in lowest terms.

7. a queen _____

8. a red card _____

9. a king or jack _____

10. a red ten _____

11. a six of diamonds _____

12. a six, seven, or eight of any suit _____

13. a nine of diamonds or hearts _____

14. a spade _____

Probability of Compound Events

Mathematicians use **probability trees** to determine the probability of compound events. When using probability trees, it is necessary to consider the probability of each outcome at each step of the experiment.

▶ Consider an experiment in which one card is drawn from each stack shown.

Stack #1   Stack #2

1. Find the theoretical probability of each event. Give each as a fraction in lowest terms.

a. P(six from Stack #1) _____   **b.** P(seven from Stack #1) _____

c. P(six from Stack #2) _____   **d.** P(seven from Stack #2) _____

A probability tree is constructed in levels. At each level, "branches" are drawn to show the possible types of outcomes for that part of the experiment. The branches are labeled with the probability for each of these outcomes.

The first level shows the two outcomes that might occur when drawing from Stack #1, along with the probability of each. The next level shows the outcomes and probabilities when drawing a card from Stack #2. The probability of each compound event is found by multiplying the probabilities along the path.

2. Fill in the missing probabilities on the diagram below.

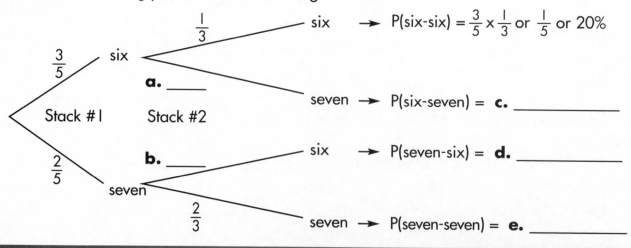

Probability of Compound Events (cont.)

3. Use the information generated by the probability tree to determine the probability for the events listed. Give your answers as percents.

a. P(two sixes) = _____

b. P(two sevens) = _____

c. P(a six with a seven) = _____

d. What is the sum of the Probabilities from a-c? _____

Why does this make sense?

▶ Consider an experiment which involves drawing one numbered tile from Bag 1 and another numbered tile from Bag 2.

4. Find the following probabilities.

a. P(even from Bag 1) = _____

b. P(odd from Bag 1) = _____

c. P(even from Bag 2) = _____

d. P(odd from Bag 2) = _____

Bag 1

| 1 | 2 |
| 3 | 4 |

Bag 2

| 5 | 6 |
| 7 | |

5. Complete the probability tree for this experiment. Fill in all the missing terms and values.

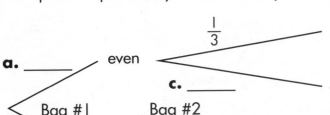
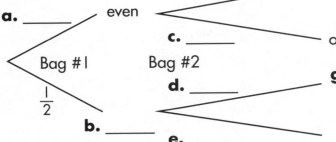

f. _____
P(even-even) = **i.** _____

a. _____ even

$\frac{1}{3}$

c. _____ odd

j. _____ = _____

Bag #1   Bag #2

d. _____

g. _____ **k.** _____ = _____

$\frac{1}{2}$

b. _____

e. _____

h. _____

P(odd-odd) = **l.** _____

6. Use your probability tree to find the theoretical probability of each event. Give each as a fraction and as a percent.

a. P(two even numbers) = _____

b. P(two odd numbers) = _____

c. P(an even number with an odd number) = _____

Answer Key

Integers...4

1. ⁻48, ⁻40, ⁻39, ⁻10, 2, 15, 39, 50
2. ⁻5,472; ⁻4,560; ⁻4,559; ⁻3,201; ⁻3,021; ⁻3,012; ⁻2,999; ⁻2891
3. True
4. True
5. False; -2 ≠ 2
6. False; 6 ≠ -6
7. True
8. False; ⁻110 ≠ 110
9. Yes
10. No 5 − 3 ≠ 3 − 5
11. Yes
12. No 6 ÷ 2 ≠ 2 ÷ 6

Addition and Subtraction with Integers 5

1.

⁻5	4	⁻1
⁻8	2	⁻6
3	2	5

2.

⁻6	2	⁻4
⁻1	⁻2	⁻3
⁻5	4	⁻1

3.

7	-3	4
5	-6	-1
2	3	5

4.

⁻3	⁻4	⁻7
4	⁻2	2
⁻7	⁻2	⁻9

5.

⁻4	⁻2	⁻6
⁻10	⁻3	⁻13
6	1	7

6.

⁻9	1	⁻8
1	⁻4	⁻3
⁻10	5	⁻5

7.

⁻4	⁻8	⁻12
⁻1	⁻6	⁻7
⁻3	⁻2	⁻5

8.

⁻4	5	1
2	⁻2	0
⁻6	7	1

Multiplication and Division with Integers......6

1.
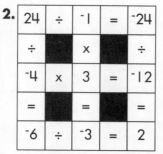

2	x	4	=	8
x		x		x
⁻1	x	⁻4	=	4
=		=		=
⁻2	x	⁻16	=	32

2.

24	÷	⁻1	=	⁻24
÷		x		÷
⁻4	x	3	=	⁻12
=		=		=
⁻6	÷	⁻3	=	2

Integers and Exponents...........................7

1. 25
2. ⁻27
3. ⁻16
4. 9
5. ⁻64
6. 4,096
7. 16
8. ⁻25
9. 81
10. $\frac{1}{25}$
11. $\frac{1}{27}$
12. $-\frac{1}{125}$
13. $-\frac{1}{32}$
14. $\frac{1}{81}$
15. $\frac{1}{36}$

Integers in Context 8

1. ⁻5 + 15 = n; Todd had $10 left.
2. ⁻25 + 8 + ⁻12 = n; The diver was at ⁻29 ft.
3. 7 + ⁻8 + 4 = n; Luisa was 3 spaces ahead of where she started.
4. ⁻150 + 70 = n; Kiyoshi still owed $80.

Equivalent Fractions..................................9

978 days

Comparing Fractions 10

SPAIN WON THE WORLD CUP

Adding Fractions 11

1. $\frac{17}{20}$
2. $1\frac{1}{10}$
3. $\frac{5}{6}$
4. $1\frac{1}{24}$
5. $\frac{50}{63}$
6. $\frac{263}{350}$
7. $7\frac{5}{8}$
8. $3\frac{13}{18}$
9. $7\frac{3}{4}$
10. $4\frac{1}{21}$
11. $13\frac{7}{18}$
12. $11\frac{1}{8}$
13. $2\frac{41}{156}$
14. $4\frac{59}{60}$
15. $4\frac{27}{40}$

Subtracting Fractions 12

KALAMAZOO, MICHIGAN

Multiplying Fractions...................................13

1. $\frac{3}{8}$
2. $\frac{8}{15}$
3. $\frac{3}{10}$
4. $\frac{6}{25}$
5. $\frac{21}{188}$
6. $16\frac{1}{2}$
7. $8\frac{5}{9}$
8. $69\frac{5}{7}$
9. $50\frac{5}{11}$
10. $39\frac{2}{3}$
11. $22\frac{3}{4}$
12. $12\frac{5}{6}$
13. $13\frac{13}{15}$
14. $65\frac{1}{3}$
15. $5\frac{15}{28}$

Dividing Fractions 14

THEY ARE BIRDS THAT CAN'T FLY!

Estimating Mixed Number Sums and Differences 15

1. F
2. C
3. D
4. A
5. B
6. E

Answer Key

Estimating Mixed Number Products and Quotients 16

1. 81	**2.** 12	**3.** 39
4. 28	**5.** 60	**6.** 7
7. 4	**8.** 15	**9.** 18
10. 9	**11.** 63	**12.** 40

Fractions and Exponents 17

1. $\frac{25}{36}$	**2.** $\frac{64}{81}$	**3.** $\frac{4}{3} = 1\frac{1}{3}$
4. $\frac{81}{100}$	**5.** $\frac{8}{27}$	**6.** $\frac{1}{32}$
7. $\frac{9}{8} = 1\frac{1}{8}$	**8.** $\frac{27}{4} = 6\frac{3}{4}$	**9.** $\frac{25}{49}$
10. $\frac{27}{64}$	**11.** $\frac{36}{25} = 1\frac{11}{25}$	**12.** $\frac{49}{25} = 1\frac{24}{25}$
13. $\frac{27}{8} = 3\frac{3}{8}$	**14.** 32	**15.** $\frac{100}{81} = 1\frac{19}{81}$

Fractions and the Associative Property 18

1. H	**2.** I	**3.** A
4. E	**5.** F	**6.** L

7. $(a + b) + c = a + (b + c)$
8. $a \times (b \times c) = (a \times b) \times c$

Fractions in Context.....................19

1. Discount = $13.32
Sale Price = $26.63
2. 3 ft. $1\frac{1}{8}$ in.
3. $9\frac{11}{12}$ square feet
4. $1\frac{1}{12}$ lb.
5. $\frac{5}{18}$

Decimals and Place Value 20
EINSWINE

Reading and Writing Decimals.....................21

DOWN
1. 32.67094
2. 918.476632
3. 2.299
4. .508056
5. .00017
9. 705.30636
11. 610.002312
12. 74.9301

ACROSS
6. 524.103812
7. 87.75034
8. .6334
10. 10.608211
13. 37.004008
14. 36.09992

Comparing and Ordering Decimals 22
FRANCIS HOPKINSON

Rounding Decimals 23
FEMALE

Adding and Subtracting Decimals 24
APOLLO THIRTEEN

Multiplying Decimals 25

1. 0.077526	**2.** 0.000351	**3.** 0.045018
4. 0.0416584	**5.** 0.0901152	**6.** 0.088352
7. 0.0055944	**8.** 0.00634	**9.** 0.0559463
10. 0.073278	**11.** 0.002552	**12.** 0.0738608

Dividing Decimals 26
HUMANS AND PIGS

Estimating Decimal Sums and Differences 27
JOEYS

Estimating Decimal Products and Quotients 28

1. G	**6.** C
2. H	**7.** B
3. F	**8.** I
4. D	**9.** A
5. E	

Managing a Checking Account 29

1. $1,378.98 − $1,050.00 = $328.98
2. $328.98 − $223.42 = $105.56
3. $105.56 − $40 = $65.56
4. $65.56 − $36.30 = $29.26
5. $29.26 − $178.46 = ⁻$149.20
6. ⁻$149.20 − $30.00 = ⁻$179.20
7. ⁻$179.20 + $523.81 = $344.61
8. $344.61 + $30.00 = $374.61
9. $374.61 − $48.23 = $326.38
10. $326.38 − $298.60 = $27.78
11. A value less than $27.78 should be in the withdrawal column.
12. A value of $523.81 should be in the deposit column. Balance will vary.

Scientific Notation 30
SKUNKEL

Fractions as Repeating Decimals 31
WILLIAM HOWARD TAFT

Answer Key

Percents, Decimals, and Fractions 32

	Percent	Decimal	Fraction
1.	50%	0.50	$\frac{1}{2}$
2.	80%	0.8	$\frac{4}{5}$
3.	33%	$0.\overline{3}$	$\frac{1}{3}$
4.	$16\frac{2}{3}\%$	$0.1\overline{6}$	$\frac{167}{1000}$
5.	2%	0.02	$\frac{1}{50}$
6.	12.5%	0.125	$\frac{1}{8}$
7.	$2\frac{1}{2}\%$	0.025	$\frac{1}{40}$
8.	72.5%	0.725	$\frac{29}{40}$
9.	40%	0.4	$\frac{2}{5}$

Mental Math: Calculating Tips 33
1. $0.90 + $0.45 = $1.35
2. $3.26 + $1.63 = $4.89
3. $4.80 + $2.40 = $7.20
4. $7.26 + $3.63 = $10.89
5. $12.00 + $6.00 = $18.00
6. $25.00 + $12.50 = $37.50
7. Move the decimal one place to the left (10%) and double it.
8. Move the decimal one place to the left (10%), triple it, and then add half of the 10% amount.

Ratios as Percents 34
1. K	2. C	3. I	4. A
5. L	6. E	7. B	8. J
9. P	10. G	11. M	12. D
13. F	14. N	15. H	16. O

Ratios in Context 35
1. 96 ft.
2. 9 cups
3. 120 seats
4. 120 people
5. 3 feet
6. 4:1

Finding Percentages 36
Path to the concert: A. 18% B. 115% E. 0.2% H. 0.8% G. 220% J. 98%
Other answers: C. 35% D. 5% F. 14% I. 9% K. 25% L. 16%

Finding the Total Number 37
ACROSS
3. eighteen
6. seventy-five
8. eighty-five
9. fifty
12. thirty-six
13. sixty
14. thirty

DOWN
1. twelve
2. seven
4. twenty-two
5. five
7. eighty-three
9. forty-eight
10. fifty-five
11. ninety-two

Percents and Proportions...........................38
THE BOXING GLOVE
Other answers: E. 40, L. 260, U. 15, S. 90, R. 8

Percent Increase and Decrease 39
1. E		7. B	
2. H		8. A	
3. F		9. L	
4. C		10. K	
5. D		11. J	
6. I		12. G	

Simple Interest 40
Use $I = prt$, P = principal, r = rate, t = years, I = interest
GENERAL DOUGLAS MACARTHUR

Compound Interest 41
Use $A = P\left(1 + \frac{r}{n}\right)^{nt}$, where A = amount, P = principal, r = rate, n = compounded, and t = years.
JULIO IGLESIAS

Commission 42
HE COACHED COLLEGE FOOTBALL

Percents in Context 43
1. He will have $925.29 in his account.
2. She made $45,600 last year.
3. She will make $240 less.
4. The painting cost $4,000,000.

Powers and Roots 44
THE LONGEST RECORDED HICCUPPING ATTACK LASTED SIXTY-FIVE YEARS

Order of Operations 45
1. 91		6. ⁻1	
2. 23.75		7. 4	
3. 59		8. 5	
4. ⁻2		9. 60	
5. ⁻5		10. 6	

Factorials..46

CHARLOTTE AMALIE

Absolute Value 47

VIDEOTAPE CASSETTE

Find the Number 48

1. 2,435   **4.** 4,254
2. 5,684   **5.** 52.43
3. 1,239   **6.** 63.45

Magic Square 49

25	1	12	7
11	8	24	2
5	10	3	27
4	26	6	9

Number Systems 50

1.

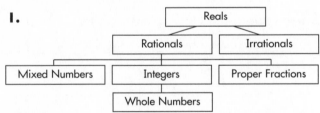

2-3.

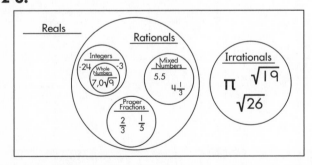

Commutative Property........................51

1. Yes. $2(A + B) = 2(B + A)$
2. No. $2(3) + 4 \neq 2(4) + 3$
3. Yes. $B^2 + A^2 = A^2 + B^2$
4. Yes. $AB + BA = BA + AB$
5. No. $3^2 - 5 \neq 5^2 - 3$
6. No. $3^4 \neq 4^3$.

Associative and Distributive Properties 52

1. associative
2. false
3. false
4. distributive
5. false
6. associative
7. distributive
8. false
9. associative
10. $6(2n) + 3(r + 2)$
     $(6 \times 2)n + 3 \times r + 3 \times 2$
     $12n + 3r + 6$
11. $(5t + 2u) + 3u + 4(v - 2)$
     $5t + (2u + 3u) + 4 \times v - 4 \times 2$
     $5t + 5u + 4v - 8$
12. $8p + (4p + t) + 2(t + 3)$
     $(8p + 4p) + t + 2 \times t + 2 \times 3$
     $12p + t + 2t + 6$
     $12p + 3t + 6$

Patterns..53

1. 27, 44 Pattern: $y + 5, y + 7$
2. 200, 220, 240 Pattern: $y + 20$
3. 106 Pattern: $y \div 2, y + 28$
4. 6,561 Pattern: y^2
5. 625, 3,125 Pattern: $5y$
6. 9, 15, 22 Pattern: it is an addition pattern with each interval increasing by one.
7. O, L, Pattern: the pattern is the alphabet in reverse, with every third letter selected.
8. Pattern: two triangles followed by two squares.

Series 54

1. 10th term: 100
     nth term: n^2
2. 10th term: 5
     nth term: $\frac{n}{2}$
3. 10th term: 1,000
     nth term: n^3
4. 10th term: 0
     nth term: $10 - n$
5. 10th term: 1,024
     nth term: 2^n
6. Answers will vary.

Answer Key

Graphs and Relationships 55
1. F   **2.** B
3. A   **4.** C
5. E   **6.** D

Graphs and Rates of Change 56
1. 1. A
  2. D
  3. C
  4. E
  5. F
  6. B
2. A. The boy fills the tub with water.
  B. The boy leaves to find the dog.
  C. The dog is put in the tub.
  D. The dog jumps out of the tub.
  E. The dog is put back in the tub.
  F. The dog jumps out of the tub.
  G. The boy dumps the water out of the tub.
3. A ferris wheel.

Solving by Substitution 57
UNIQUE UP ON HIM
THE TAME WAY

Equations: Checking Solutions 58
Homer's path should follow the boxes containing these
solutions:
$y = 22$, $x = 18$ $b = {}^-10$, $m = 63$, $a = 8$, $x = 3$, $c = 27$,
$c = 59$, $a = 75$ $y = {}^-7$, $a = {}^-9$, $b = 3$, $x = 8$, $c = {}^-44$,
$w = -30$, $y = 9$, $x = 13$, and $c = 46$

Solving 1-Step Equations 59
WOMEN'S ICE HOCKEY

Solving Equations: Scrambled Steps............60
1. B, D, A, C, E
2. E, B, D, A, C
3. D, C, A, E, B
4. B, A, E, C, D

Equations Involving Two Operations 61
  1. $x = 35$ **2.** $r = 25$ **3.** $n = {}^-63$
  4. $p = {}^-8$ **5.** $b = {}^-35$ **6.** $a = 44$
  7. $s = 60$ **8.** $c = 56$ **9.** $y = {}^-60$
  10. $m = {}^-15$ **11.** $c = 108$ **12.** $r = {}^-45$
  13. $y = {}^-12$ **14.** $c = 22$ **15.** $x = {}^-84$

Functions: Checking Solutions 62
PEREGRINE FALCON

Coordinate Grids: Quadrants.....................63
  1. II   **2.** I   **3.** origin
  4. x-axis   **5.** y-axis   **6.** III
  7. II   **8.** I & IV   **9.** y-axis
  10. x-axis   **11.** y-axis and II   **12.** III & IV
  13. II & III   **14.** III & IV   **15.** I & II
  16. I & IV   **17.** I & II   **18.** I & III
  19. I & IV   **20.** II & IV

Slope Between Two Points..........................64
  1. $\frac{5}{4}$ **2.** ${}^-1$ **3.** 0
  4. positive slope   **5.** negative slope   **6.** $\frac{2}{3}$
  7. $-\frac{2}{3}$ **8.** ${}^-5$

The Distance Formula 65
  1. 5.00   **2.** 13.00
  3. 11.18   **4.** 15.00
  5. 17.00   **6.** 10.00
  7. 2.24   **8.** 6.00
  9. 6.71   **10.** 11.18

Linear Equations: Finding Intercepts............66

1.

x	y
0	2
3	0

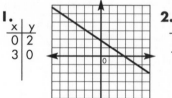

2.

x	y
0	2
-5	0

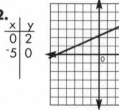

3.

x	y
0	-1
5	0

 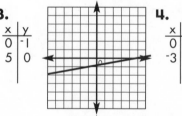

4.

x	y
0	3
-3	0

5.

x	y
0	-4
-1	0

 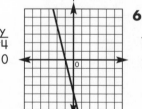

6.

x	y
0	3
1	0

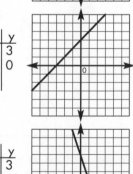 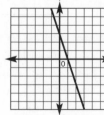

Linear Equations: Slope-Intercept Form 67

1.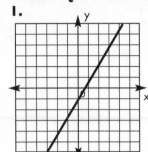

2.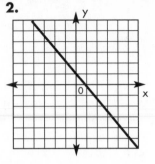

3.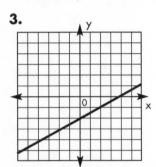

4.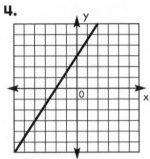

Linear Equations: Graphs...........................68

1. E, O
2. H, J
3. A, K
4. D, N

5. B, P
6. F, M
7. C, L
8. G, I

Parallel and Perpendicular Lines 69

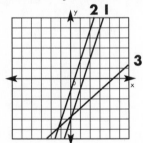

4. Equations 1 and 2 have the same slope. The lines are parallel.
5. Equations 1 and 3 have the same y-intercept.

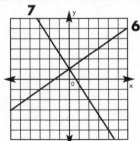

8. Lines 6 and 7 are perpendicular.
9. The slopes of graphs 6 and 7 are opposite reciprocals.

Systems of Equations.....................................70

1. (-7, 7) **2.** (-4, 8) **3.** (-1, 5) **4.** (2, 4)
5. (7, 1) **6.** (9, -3) **7.** (3, -9) **8.** (-2, -10)
9. (-3, -6) **10.** (-10, -5)

Points should be connected in the following order: sushi bar, garden, beach, ice-cream parlor, basketball court, apple orchard, lemonade stand, pond, church, and pig farm.

Equations in Context 71

1. a. $C = .05p + 0.065p + p = 1.115p$
   b. $269.06
2. a. Agency 1: $C = 50 + 0.25m$
       Agency 2: $C = 40 + 0.40m$
   b. If you travel 115 miles, agency 1 is the better deal. If you travel 65 miles, agency 2 is the better deal.
   c. Use agency 2 if you plan on traveling less than 66.7 miles. Use agency 1 if you plan on traveling more than 66.7 miles.
3. a. Golden Hammer: $C = 0.15p$
       Heavy Gavel: $C = 500 + 0.12p$
   b. The commission at Golden Hammer would be $3,750 and at Heavy Gavel it would be $3,500. Heavy Gavel would be the best choice.

Building Expressions 72

1. $I + T + I + T + I + T + I + T$
2. $T + (T + 2) + T + (T + 2)$
3. $(T + I) + (T + I) + (T + I) + (T + I)$
4. $(T + 2) + T + I + T + I + T$
5. Each expression simplifies to $4T + 4$.
6. a. 16
   b. 20
   c. 24
   d. 28
   e. 44

Critical Thinking...73

1. $\frac{1}{4}$ inch. The front cover of Vol. 2 would be next to the back cover of Vol. 1 so Booky only burrowed through the two bindings ($\frac{1}{8} + \frac{1}{8}$).
2. The first trucker took longer (you can not average the rates because the times are different).
3. As you try to walk home, you will actually move a step towards the school. 300 steps later, you will be at the school.
4. It cannot be done. One lap at 30 mph takes 2 min. To average 60 mph for two laps, the driver needs to travel the two laps in 2 min. He would have to take the second lap in zero time.
5. 6 sec/5 = $1\frac{1}{5}$ sec. When a clock strikes 12:00 there are 11 "time slots" compared to 5 "time slots" for 6:00, so the time would be more than double - 13 $\frac{1}{5}$ sec.
6. 29 days -it would double to cover the pond on day 30.

Answer Key

Classifying Objects 74

I.

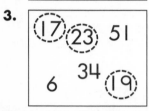

Criteria: closed, rounded and straight edges

2.

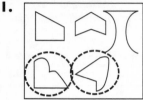

Criteria: letters made of straight line segments

3.

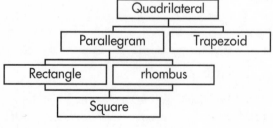

Criteria: prime numbers

4. Answers will vary.

Identifying Geometric Terms 75

1. H
2. A
3. D
4. F
5. G

6. B
7. E
8. C
9. I
10. J

Angle Sums and Triangles 76

A. 60°	**G.** 90°	**M.** 150°	**S.** 60°
B. 120°	**H.** 90°	**N.** 30°	**T.** 120°
C. 60°	**I.** 120°	**O.** 150°	**U.** 150°
D. 120°	**J.** 60°	**P.** 30°	**V.** 30°
E. 90°	**K.** 120°	**Q.** 60°	**W.** 150°
F. 90°	**L.** 60°	**R.** 120°	**X.** 30°

Quadrilaterals 77

Quadrilateral

Parallegram   Trapezoid

Rectangle   rhombus

Square

1. All
2. Some
3. No
4. Some
5. Some

6. All
7. All
8. All
9. All
10. No

Parts of a Circle...78

1. G	**6.** C	**11.** H
2. B	**7.** I	**12.** J
3. G	**8.** H	**13.** J
4. D	**9.** E	**14.** A
5. F	**10.** B	**15.** F

Classifying Polyhedrons...............................79

1. hexagonal prism
2. triangular prism
3. square prism
4. square pyramid
5. triangular pyramid

6. hexagonal pyramid
7. pentagonal prism
8. rectangular pyramid
9. trapezoidal prism

Similar Triangles 80

1. $m\angle A = m\angle D = 48°$
$m\angle B = 67°$, $m\angle F = 65°$.
$b = 10.5$, $f = 4.3$

2. $m\angle C = 90°$, $m\angle D = 30°$.
$m\angle B = m\angle E = 60°$
$a = 3$, $c = 5$, $e = 20$

3. $m\angle A = m\angle D = 60°$
$m\angle B = 30°$
$b = 7.5$, $c = 12.5$,

4. $m\angle A = m\angle D = m\angle F = 62°$
$m\angle E = 56°$
$c = a = 20$

Similar Figures and Perimeter 81

1. $P = 18$
2. $P = 9$
3. $a = 6$
4. ratio $= \frac{3}{10}$
5. $P = 9$
6. ratio $= \frac{2}{7}$

Pythagorean Theorem 82

1. $c = 13$ **2.** $c = 8.49$ **3.** $c = 15$
4. $a = 24$ **5.** $b = 20$ **6.** $a = 30$

Angle Sums of Polygons 83

1. 360°
3. 900°
5. 360°
7. 1,620°
9. $T = N - 2$

2. 720°
4. 1,080°
6. 900°
8. 1,080°
10. $180°(N - 2)$

0-7424-1723-9 *Math*

Transformations 84

1. reflection **2.** rotation **3.** translation
4. rotation **5.** rotation **6.** rotation
7. rotation **8.** reflection
9. reflection **10.** translation

Rotation Around an Axis 85

1.
4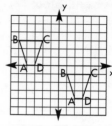

3.
4.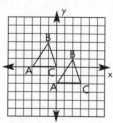

Coordinate Grid Transformations..............86

1.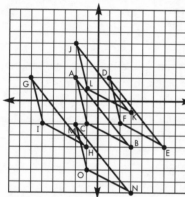

2. D(1, 2) E(6, -4) F(2, -2)
3. △DEF is △ABC translated three units to the right.
4. G(-6, 2) H (-1, -4) I(-5, -2)
5. △GHI is △ABC translated four units to the left.
6. J(-2, 5) K(3, -1) L(-1, 1)
7. △JKL is △ABC translated three units upwards.
8. M(-2, -2) N(3, -8) O(-1, -6)
9. △MNO is △ABC translated four units downwards

Coordinate Grid Transformations..............87

1.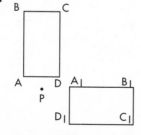
2.

3.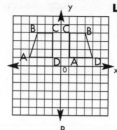
4.

5.

6.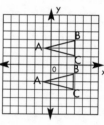

Point of View 88

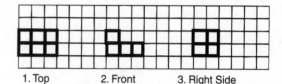

1. Top   2. Front   3. Right Side

4.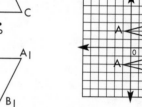

5.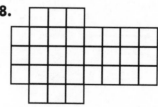

Nets 89

1. C **2.** A **3.** B
4. 22 cm² **5.** 16 cm² **6.** 14 cm²
7. C
8.

Area: 30 cm²

Answer Key

Perimeter and Area: Triangles and Trapezoids 90
1. half
2. $\frac{1}{2}$
3. 18 cm²
4. 112 mm²
5. 24 in.²
6. plus
7. +
8. +
9. 375 mm²
10. 108 in.²
11. 3 ft.²

Circumference and Area of Circles 91
1. C = 25.12 in.
A = 50.24 in.²
2. C = 314 mm
A = 7,850 mm²
3. C = 9.42 in.
A = 7.07 in.²
4. C = 62.80 ft.
A = 314 ft.²
5. C = 5.02 cm
A = 2.01 cm²
6. C = 1.57 mm
A = 0.20 mm²
7. C = 125.60 mm
A = 1,256 mm²
8. C = 47.10 in.
A = 176.63 in.²
9. C = 13.19 m
A = 13.85 m²
Use π = 3.14

Area of Irregular Shapes 92
1. 816 in.²
2. 648 ft.²
3. 120 ft.²
4. 272.97 in.²
5. 13.08 in.²
6. 67.2 in.²
7. 10.52 in.²
8. 3.46 in.²
9. 9.42 ft.²
10. 3.44 in.² greater.

Volume of Prisms and Cylinders 93
1. 1,050 cm³
2. 32 m³
3. 12.768 ft.³
4. 1,904 mm³
5. 2,373.84 cm³
6. 141.3 m³
7. 351.68 cm³
8. 113.04 mm³
9. 339.12 ft.³
Use π = 3.14

Volume of Pyramids and Cones..................94
1. 120 ft.³
2. 200 ft.³
3. 80 ft.³
4. 5 cm³
5. 4,308.08 ft.³
6. 65.94 cm³

Surface Area 95
1. 132 ft.²
2. 880 ft.²
3. 282 mm²
4. 112 cm²
5. 120 m²
6. 99 m²

Scale Factors: Area 96
1. a. w = 6 cm; l = 18 cm
   b. 12 cm²
   c. 108 cm²
   d. 9
2. a. b = 20 in.; h = 8 in.
   b. 5 in.²
   c. 80 in.²
   d. 16
3. 25
4. k^2
5. 1,800 cm²
6. 640 cm²

Scale Factors: Volume 97
1. a. w = 12 cm; l = 12 cm; h = 18 cm
   b. 96 cm³
   c. 2,592 cm³
   d. 27
2. a. w = 8 cm; l = 8 cm; h = 12 cm
   b. 4 cm³
   c. 256 cm³
   d. 64
3. 125
4. k^3
5. 27,000cm³
6. 5,120cm³

Scale Factors in Context......................98
1. a. 40 ft. by 20 ft. by 80 ft.
   b. 8,000 ft.²
   c. 64,000 ft.³
2. a. 50 ft. by 25 ft. by 100 ft.
   b. 12,500 ft.²
   c. 125,000 ft.³
3. a. The dimensions of the building will be k times bigger than those of the scale model.
   h = 4k; w = k; l = 2k
   b. The area of the building walls will be k^2 times bigger than that of the scale model.
   A = 20k²
   c. The volume of the building will be k^3 times bigger than that of the scale model.
   V = 8k³

Measurement in Context 99
1. a. 2,506 cm²
   b. The larger poster board is the better deal.
2. a. No. The box holds 7,776 cubic inches of material. The cylindrical container only holds 5,528 cubic inches.
   b. The box holds 2,548 more cubic inches of material.
3. a. 6.4 panels
   b. 4 panels
   c. The smaller panels, at $11.44 per square foot, are a better deal than the larger panels, which cost $11.87 per square foot.
4. 1,600 cubic inches

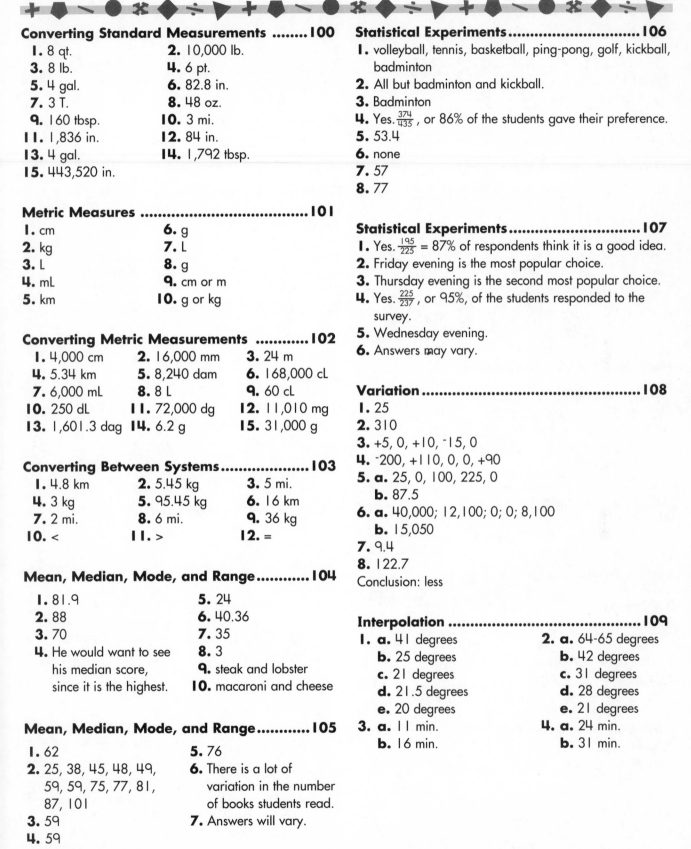

Converting Standard Measurements 100

1. 8 qt.
2. 10,000 lb.
3. 8 lb.
4. 6 pt.
5. 4 gal.
6. 82.8 in.
7. 3 T.
8. 48 oz.
9. 160 tbsp.
10. 3 mi.
11. 1,836 in.
12. 84 in.
13. 4 gal.
14. 1,792 tbsp.
15. 443,520 in.

Metric Measures 101

1. cm
6. g
2. kg
7. L
3. L
8. g
4. mL
9. cm or m
5. km
10. g or kg

Converting Metric Measurements 102

1. 4,000 cm
2. 16,000 mm
3. 24 m
4. 5.34 km
5. 8,240 dam
6. 168,000 cL
7. 6,000 mL
8. 8 L
9. 60 cL
10. 250 dL
11. 72,000 dg
12. 11,010 mg
13. 1,601.3 dag
14. 6.2 g
15. 31,000 g

Converting Between Systems....................103

1. 4.8 km
2. 5.45 kg
3. 5 mi.
4. 3 kg
5. 95.45 kg
6. 16 km
7. 2 mi.
8. 6 mi.
9. 36 kg
10. <
11. >
12. =

Mean, Median, Mode, and Range............104

1. 81.9
5. 24
2. 88
6. 40.36
3. 70
7. 35
4. He would want to see his median score, since it is the highest.
8. 3
9. steak and lobster
10. macaroni and cheese

Mean, Median, Mode, and Range............105

1. 62
5. 76
2. 25, 38, 45, 48, 49, 59, 59, 75, 77, 81, 87, 101
6. There is a lot of variation in the number of books students read.
3. 59
7. Answers will vary.
4. 59

Statistical Experiments.............................106

1. volleyball, tennis, basketball, ping-pong, golf, kickball, badminton
2. All but badminton and kickball.
3. Badminton
4. Yes. $\frac{374}{435}$, or 86% of the students gave their preference.
5. 53.4
6. none
7. 57
8. 77

Statistical Experiments.............................107

1. Yes. $\frac{195}{225}$ = 87% of respondents think it is a good idea.
2. Friday evening is the most popular choice.
3. Thursday evening is the second most popular choice.
4. Yes. $\frac{225}{237}$, or 95%, of the students responded to the survey.
5. Wednesday evening.
6. Answers may vary.

Variation 108

1. 25
2. 310
3. +5, 0, +10, ⁻15, 0
4. ⁻200, +110, 0, 0, +90
5. a. 25, 0, 100, 225, 0
   b. 87.5
6. a. 40,000; 12,100; 0; 0; 8,100
   b. 15,050
7. 9.4
8. 122.7
Conclusion: less

Interpolation 109

1. a. 41 degrees
   b. 25 degrees
   c. 21 degrees
   d. 21.5 degrees
   e. 20 degrees
2. a. 64-65 degrees
   b. 42 degrees
   c. 31 degrees
   d. 28 degrees
   e. 21 degrees
3. a. 11 min.
   b. 16 min.
4. a. 24 min.
   b. 31 min.

Answer Key

Double Line and Bar Graphs 110

1.

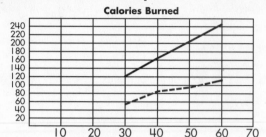

Calories Burned

2.

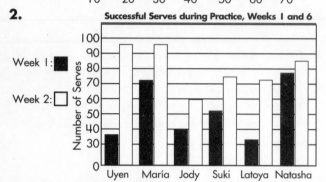

Successful Serves during Practice, Weeks 1 and 6

Week 1: ■
Week 2: □

Frequency Tables and Histograms 111

1.

Fran's Frequency Table

Distribution of Flea Market Items

Price Intervals	Tally	Frequency
$1 – $5	ЖЖ III	8
$6 – $10	ЖЖ IIII	9
$11 – $15	ЖЖ I	6
$16 – $20	IIII	4
$21 – $25	ЖЖ	5
$26 – $30	III	3
$31 – $35	I	1
$36 – $40	IIII	4

2.

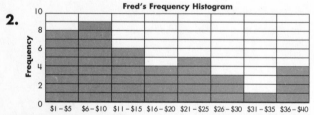

Fred's Frequency Histogram

3. greatest: $6 – $10
least: $31 – $35

Quartiles 112

1. 45, 55, 59, 62, 67, 68, 70, 72, 75, 76, 77, 80, 81, 85, 88, 89, 91, 95, 100
2. 76
3. 67
4. 88
5. No
6. 19
7. 14
8. 73.7%
9. 74th ; 73.7
10. **a.** 1st: 76, 2nd: 82; 3rd: 93
    b. 91st percentile

Box Plots 113

A.

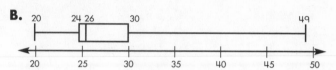

B.

C. Box plot A has more variation, since there is a larger range between the 1st and 3rd quartiles. They both have the same median and extreme values.

Probability 114

1. $\frac{7}{12}$, 0.583, 58.3% **4.** $\frac{11}{12}$, 0.917, 91.7%

2. 0, 0, 0% **5.** $\frac{1}{3}$, 0.333, 33.3%

3. $\frac{1}{12}$, 0.083, 8.3% **6.** $\frac{5}{12}$, 0.417, 41.7%

Probability 115

1. $\frac{1}{6}$	**8.** $\frac{1}{2}$
2. $\frac{1}{12}$	**9.** $\frac{2}{13}$
3. $\frac{1}{8}$	**10.** $\frac{1}{26}$
4. $\frac{1}{9}$	**11.** $\frac{1}{52}$
5. $\frac{6}{36}$, $\frac{1}{6}$	**12.** $\frac{3}{13}$
6. $\frac{5}{36}$	**13.** $\frac{1}{26}$
7. $\frac{1}{13}$	**14.** $\frac{1}{4}$

Probability of Compound Events 116–117

1. a. $\frac{3}{5}$ **4. a.** $\frac{1}{2}$
   b. $\frac{2}{5}$ **b.** $\frac{1}{2}$
   c. $\frac{1}{3}$ **c.** $\frac{1}{3}$
   d. $\frac{2}{3}$ **d.** $\frac{2}{3}$

2. a. $\frac{2}{3}$ **5. a.** $\frac{1}{2}$
   b. $\frac{1}{3}$ **b.** odd
   c. $\frac{3}{5} \times \frac{2}{3} = \frac{2}{5} = 40\%$ **c.** $\frac{2}{3}$
   d. $\frac{2}{5} \times \frac{1}{3} = \frac{2}{15} = 13\%$ **d.** $\frac{1}{3}$
   e. $\frac{2}{5} \times \frac{2}{3} = \frac{4}{15} = 27\%$ **e.** $\frac{2}{3}$
                                f. even
3. a. 20%   **g.** even
   b. 27%   **h.** odd
   c. 53%   **i.** P(even-even) = $\frac{1}{6}$ = 17%
   d. 100%. Yes, each   **j.** P(even-odd) = $\frac{1}{3}$ = 33%
      probability is an   **k.** P(odd-even) = $\frac{1}{6}$ = 17%
      independent event, all   **l.** P(odd-odd) = $\frac{1}{3}$ = 33%
      possible independent   **6. a.** $\frac{1}{6}$ = 17%
      events for a situation   **b.** $\frac{1}{3}$ = 33%
      should add up to   **c.** $\frac{1}{3} + \frac{1}{6}$ = 50%
      100%.

0-7424-1723-9 *Math*